The Great Collaboration

The Great Collaboration

The First 100 Years of the Association of Official Analytical Chemists

KENNETH HELRICH

Research Professor, Rutgers, the State University of New Jersey

Published in conjunction with the 100th anniversary
of the Association of Official Analytical Chemists

1884-1984
AOAC

The Association of Official Analytical Chemists, Inc.
1111 North 19th Street, Suite 210
Arlington, Virginia 22209 USA

Copyright 1984 by the Association of Official Analytical Chemists, Inc.

Library of Congress Cataloging in Publication Data

Helrich, Kenneth, 1924–
    The great collaboration.
    "Published in conjunction with the 100th anniversary
of the Association of Official Analytical Chemists."
Bibliography: p.
Includes index.
1. Association of Official Analyical Chemists—
History. I. Association of Official Analytical Chemists.
II. Title
QD71.A853H45 1984   543'.006'073
83-21365
ISBN 0-935584-25-0

To Alice

PREFACE

The Association of Official Analytical Chemists (formerly Agricultural Chemists), founded in September 1884, is celebrating its centennial.

A one hundredth birthday is always an auspicious occasion. When it marks the beginning of a second century of service, growth, and technical advancement for an organization, it is also a period of nostalgia and enormous pride for its members and advocates. At such a time, it seems appropriate to gather together the bits and pieces that stand as a record of past events and set them down in an orderly fashion so that we can examine where we came from, why, and what we have accomplished. We may even acquire from this process some sense of where we should be heading in the future.

In attempting to recount the events of a century, it quickly becomes apparent that a great many individuals played significant roles in the affairs of AOAC. To give due credit to everyone in this account would be an impossibility; at the same time, the omission of the names of individuals associated with particular episodes would result in a dry recital of facts. For this reason, the author must apologize to those members, past and present, who have contributed greatly to the success of AOAC but whose recognition may have been overlooked in this narrative. The Association has been unusually blessed with members who have contributed unstintingly to its success during its entire history.

The author extends thanks to Dr. William Horwitz for initially suggesting this "history project" and for his helpful comments and review of the manuscript. Ms. Helen Reynolds reviewed the manuscript in several stages, made numerous valuable suggestions, and provided moral support and encouragement, all of which were appreciated.

Thanks are also due to the following who contributed recollections, anecdotes, and other firsthand information which proved invaluable in telling this story: Daniel Banes, Richard Blakely, Harold Egan, Frederick Garfield, Eugene H. Holeman, Wallace F. Janssen, Bernhard Larsen, David B. MacLean, W. Perce McKinley, Alex Mathers, Lessel Ramsey, Robert C. Rund, Elwyn D. Schall, Peter M. Scott, and Michael Wehr.

The author is indebted to the Rutgers University Faculty Academic Study Program for the opportunity to spend the considerable time required to research and write this history. The courtesies and help of the AOAC staff are also gratefully acknowledged. They did much to make this project a pleasant experience.

The *Proceedings* of the early meetings of the Convention of Agricultural Chemists, beginning in May 1880 and continuing through the organizational meeting in 1884, provided much information on the formation of the Association. *Proceedings* of the meetings of AOAC, printed in the annual reports of the Division and later Bureau of Chemistry of the U.S. Department of Agriculture (USDA), were used extensively as source material, as well as the 66 volumes of the *Journal of the AOAC*.

Other references used are listed in the bibliography.

CONTENTS

In the Beginning

When one considers the wide scope of interests and the sophisticated activities of AOAC in its hundredth year of existence, its modest beginnings arbitrating methods of analysis for three fertilizer elements do indeed seem to be in the very distant past. However, the growth and progress of AOAC has paralleled that of the consumer protection movement and of scientific technology. It has provided leaders in both fields.

In the latter part of the nineteenth century, scientific agriculture was in its infancy, as was the science of agricultural chemistry. This was particularly true in North America. The pioneering work in organic chemistry, and consequently agricultural chemistry, had been done in Europe by such illustrious scientists as Liebig, Fresenius, Voit, Hoffman, and Pasteur, as well as Sir Humphrey Davy who wrote the first noteworthy book in the English language on *Elements of Agricultural Chemistry* in 1813. The main emphasis in United States colleges at the time was on the study of classics, and American students wishing advanced instruction in agricultural chemistry (or any science) were obliged to travel to Europe. As late as 1908 at the twenty-fifth annual convention of AOAC, President Snyder pointed out that most of the original members had been trained in European laboratories, many of them as students of the pioneers mentioned above. He urged that we, in America, should increase special training in agricultural chemistry in all areas including analytical. Despite the limited learning facilities at home, there was still a core group of fine agricultural chemists in this country in the late 1800s.

There were also the beginnings of the fine training and research facilities that have since become world leaders in progressive agriculture. The first president of AOAC, Samuel W. Johnson, began his study of chemistry at the New School of Applied Science at Yale in 1850. He then continued to study for two years abroad with leaders in chemistry and agricultural sciences such as Erdman and Neumann in Leipzig, Pettenkoffer and von Kobel in Munich, and Frankland, Larves, and Gilbert in England. On his return in August 1855, he became a professor and researcher in the newly organized Scientific School at Yale. At the same time, he lectured and wrote articles on topics in scientific agriculture which were publicized in *Agricultural Society* and other publications. He was a champion of the idea of commercial valuation of fertilizer materials, since the concept of checking fraud and evaluating deficiencies in plant food in terms of money (with the possibility of a monetary adjustment between buyer and seller) was of interest to practical farmers. Commercial valuation provided them with an understanding of the value of scientific research, nutrient analysis in particular, and helped gain their support for scientific agriculture.

The Federal Land Grant Act of 1862 was passed during the period of Johnson's public activity in behalf of scientific agriculture, and the Scientific School at Yale became the Sheffield Scientific School, the institution designated by the legislature to be the land grant college in Connecticut and to receive the funds provided by the Act. Other land grant colleges were established under the Act and the emphasis on agriculture and the mechanical arts was increasing when a national convention in Washington was called in 1872 by the U.S. Commissioner of Agriculture, Frederick Watts. It was attended by about 100 leaders in agricultural chemistry and scientific agriculture from all over the country. This meeting stimulated a great deal of interest in the idea of establishing an experiment station system as a matter of national policy. Under Johnson's guidance, Connecticut gained the distinction of establishing in 1875 the first experiment station in the United States. The station was established first as a private enterprise controlled by Wesleyan University under Professor Atwater, one of Professor Johnson's former students, but it was transferred to New Haven two years later when it became a state institution. Professor Johnson was then appointed director of this first state agricultural experiment station. Other states designated land grant colleges and established experiment stations rapidly, and the movement for serious agricultural research was soon well underway.

By this time, many states had already enacted fertilizer laws, and the analysis of fertilizers by chemists in the experiment stations became one of their important duties, along with a myriad of other functions including soil research and studies on feed and food nutrition. Most of the methodology for analysis of fertilizers had been devised in the classical chemistry laboratories of Europe and had not been standardized or made uniform. Methods of sampling also varied greatly and no definitive studies in uniform sampling had been undertaken. The first collaborative type of testing of methodology for uniformity was done in one of the German experiment stations in 1872 when 19 chemists held a conference and came to an agreement on methods of analysis for phosphoric acid. In 1880, the results of fertilizer analyses by several chemists were reported, but no action was taken to adopt a method. Numerous other conferences were reported in the literature, but none constituted a true collaborative study in the AOAC sense. Also there were many early European reports of agreements on uniform fertilizer methods, but no concerted work was done in testing such methods.

Consequently, the chemists charged with analyzing fertilizer materials in the late 1800s, when states were passing laws and issuing regulations to

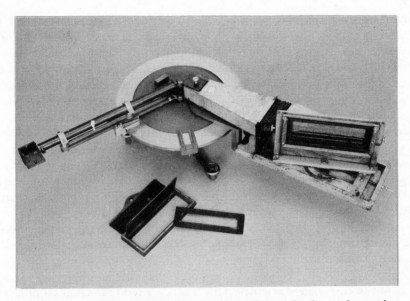

Quartz spectrograph of W.H. Hartley, 1878, used to study ultraviolet spark spectra (Crown Copyright, Science Museum, London).

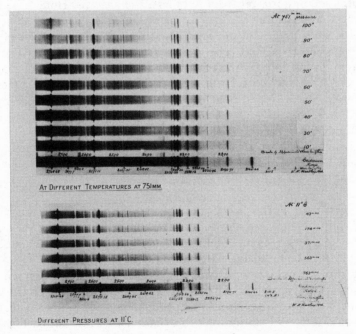

Spectra of toluene, measured by W.H. Hartley on quartz spectrograph, 1878 (Crown Copyright, Science Museum, London).

assure fair trade practices, were faced with a dilemma. The various methods of analysis available from German, French, and English agricultural chemists gave analytical results that were not comparable to each other and were not sufficiently precise for analysts to duplicate each other's results. In some cases, definitions were unclear or nonexistent; thus the chemist did not know specifically what form or forms of a nutrient to determine. Methods of sampling were not specified. With specific valuations being placed on the various nutrients, the chemist was faced with a serious financial responsibility to clients or constituents. A very slight difference in a chemical analysis for a nutrient could amount to a difference of a considerable sum of money in large-quantity fertilizer consignments. Obviously, the "company" or "seller" chemist was using the method which would give the highest possible results, while the "buyer" chemist might be using a method which would yield lower values. The official or regulatory chemist was caught in the middle, and much time was devoted to disputes over the analytical data reported in fertilizer inspections.

It was in this chaotic scientific climate that several meetings culminating in the organization of AOAC took place, beginning on May 20, 1880. Recognizing the need for someone to take the initiative in formalizing standards and uniform procedures for fertilizer analysis, Hon. J. T. Henderson, the Commissioner of Agriculture of Georgia, convened a meeting of commissioners of agriculture, representatives of the state boards of agriculture, state chemists, and professors of chemistry at state universities and state agricultural colleges in those states using large amounts of commercial fertilizers. They met on July 28, 1880, in Washington, DC, in facilities of the United States Department of Agriculture (USDA) provided by W.G. LeDuc, the Commissioner. Of the 20 attendees listed in the minutes, three were from USDA, nine were chemists from individual states, two were state commissioners of agriculture, and six appeared to be industrial chemists. Professor S. W. Johnson of Connecticut was not present but sent a letter endorsing the purpose of the meeting.

The first item on the program established for the meeting was a decision on the rights of those present to participate in a discussion of various topics and to vote on the recommendations reached. In this regard, it was decided that only practicing analytical chemists (which included all the attendees except three) would be entitled to vote on the "final judgment of the meeting." The five technical items for discussion and action on the program were methods of estimating soluble phosphoric acid, estimating "reverted" phosphoric acid, estimating insoluble phosphoric acid, estimating nitrogen (including nitrates), and estimating potash. The method of arriving at commercial valuations of fertilizers was also considered proper for discussion, if time allowed. A committee system was adopted almost immediately. The committee to consider the phosphoric acid methods and the committee to consider the nitrogen and potash methods each consisted of five of the delegates, who discussed the problems and reported their conclusions at 7:00 p.m. that same day. It was agreed to provisionally adopt methods for determination of phosphoric acid, nitrogen, and potash in commercial manures, and the recommended methods were referred to a committee of two to write the details and send the methods to all convention delegates. The methods so adopted were selected from those which had been published in various European journals, with minor modifications. The subject of setting valuations on fertilizers was discussed at length, but no action was taken.

During the discussions, it was suggested that with so many agricultural chemists present, this would be a good time and place to form a permanent organization for the purpose of meeting from time to time to discuss topics of interest to the profession. A motion was adopted that the "convention form a section in the subdivision of chemistry in the American Association for the Advancement of Science and that their next meeting be held in Boston during the regular meeting of the aforesaid association." The second meeting of the so-called "Convention of Agricultural Chemists" was held in Boston, Massachusetts, on August 27, 1880. Dr. C.A. Goessman, of the Massachusetts Agricultural College at Amherst, presided, with about 25 delegates present. After the provisional adoption for two years of the methods which had been circulated by the committee of two, there was considerable discussion concerning the advantages of a permanent organization, type of affiliation, choice of a name, etc. It was generally agreed that, for the present at least, the formation of a subsection of the American Association for the Advancement of Science (AAAS) would be a satisfactory arrangement. A suggestion that the group unite with botanists, practical agriculturalists, and others to form a subsection of agricultural sciences (instead of simply organizing as agricultural chemists) was not approved. It was pointed out that a club of scientific agriculturists was already being formed but would not conflict with one devoted to chemical work in agriculture. It was noted that a movement was underway to form a section of chemistry in AAAS and suggested that this objective might be more easily obtained by showing that chemists were ready not only to form such a section, but also to form a subsection of agricultural chemistry. A committee was appointed to "take such steps as may be necessary for securing the formation of a permanent chemical section in AAAS, and the establishment of a subsection of agricultural chemistry in such a permanent section, should it be formed."

It was in this meeting that the beginning of the concept of what developed into AOAC collaborative studies was first discussed. The delegates felt that the methods endorsed by the convention would be considered binding by other chemists throughout the country, but that actual experiments should be made to "fully establish the fitness of the methods proposed at the Washington meeting." Although the chemists might still depend more or less on the ideas and experiments of the European chemists for some time, they should begin to do more experimental work on their own "even if we do nothing more than confirm the results of Fresenius, Neubauer and Luck, and others." Dr. A.R. LeDoux of the North Carolina Experiment Station suggested that the collection and examination of published methods with subsequent adoption and reduction to one system, after careful experimental testing, would give the actions of the Convention an authority which would be generally accepted. Since there was a strong expression of interest among the delegates in participating in any experiments to perfect a scheme of fertilizer analysis, a committee of five was appointed to conduct the study of methods and report at the next meeting of the Convention, to be held in 1881, again in conjunction with AAAS.

The third meeting of the Convention of Agricultural Chemists, with 32 attendees, was held in Cincinnati, Ohio, on August 18, 1881, in the meeting hall assigned to the chemical section of AAAS. It was reported that comparatively few complaints had been received on the methods for potash and nitrogen since the Washington meeting, but the insoluble or "reverted" phosphoric acid determination had shown great discrepancies when the citrate method was used. Dr. C.U. Shephard of South Carolina had even sent out five collaborative samples of prepared artificial fertilizers to various agricultural chemists, whose results for the insoluble phosphoric acid determined by the recommended method were "simply ludicrous." The results of this first "collaborative study" were apparently never published but were circulated among the delegates. Delegates representing the fertilizer manufacturers argued that the oxalate method, which gave higher values, was far more dependable and fair. Since the previous conventions had endorsed the recommended methods provisionally for one year, there were no authorized or official methods and a change could easily have been made, but many control chemists opposed use of the oxalate method. After a great deal of discussion, a motion to adopt the oxalate method for one year was passed in spite of the opposition, and a committee was appointed to continue the investigation of the whole subject of the determination of insoluble phosphoric acid and to compare the various methods in use.

At the meeting, the "Committee on Permanent Organization" reported that their efforts to establish a section of chemistry in AAAS were near a successful conclusion and it would probably be organized the next day, making way for establishment of a subsection of agricultural chemistry. A motion that this committee was to be continued, with full power to act, was passed, and the meeting was adjourned after a contributed paper and committee reports were read. The delegates agreed to meet again, on call by the chairman, if a meeting was thought necessary before their organization as a subsection of AAAS.

The interest in at least formal collaboration by the agricultural chemists in seeking uniformity in methodology and pursuing other mutual interests seemed to die out after the closing of the 1881 meeting in Cincinnati. Dr. Harvey Wiley commented on the situation almost 20 years later: "There was a certain feeling of antipathy -- perhaps it is not well to make it so strong as this, but a strong feeling of incongruity -- existing between the trade chemists on one hand and the official chemists on the other. It was an unvoiced sentiment pervading the organization to the effect that an association composed of trade chemists and official chemists contained elements of instability which would prevent it from ever becoming highly useful." What had actually occurred was that official chemists would not accept the oxalate method.

Commissioner Henderson again took the initiative, following up the movement which he had begun and which appeared to promise to serve an extremely useful purpose. After almost three years had elapsed with apparently little or no visible activity in the furtherance of methodology cooperation, he issued a call for a meeting of the agricultural chemists to be held in the senate chamber at the Capitol in Atlanta, Georgia, on May 15, 1884. Commissioner Henderson addressed the meeting at the opening session, stressing his faith in the ability and integrity of the chemist, and pointing out the myriad of problems he had had as a control official trying to cope with varying analytical results due to differences in methods commonly in use. He reviewed the work of the previous meetings and lauded the results, expressing his hope that the present meeting would further the efforts toward uniform, satisfactory methods of analysis, and that such could be established for the next season. Henderson was then elected permanent chairman of the meeting. Departing from the previous policy that "only those who are practicing analytical chemists be considered entitled to vote," a motion was passed stating that "all of the agricultural chemists and officers of experiment stations and agricultural bureaus present be considered as members of this meeting and that they be requested to hand their names and addresses to the Secretary." Thirty members were enrolled, including Professor Harvey Washington Wiley, the chief chemist of the Bureau of Chemistry of USDA, about whom much more will be said later.

Dr. Charles U. Shephard, a commercial chemist from Charleston, South Carolina, addressed the Convention and again stressed the inconsistencies in agricultural chemical analyses and the fact that "they pinch all of us, there is no doubt." In stressing the damage that the chemist might cause to an innocent individual because of honest differences due to diverse methods, he cited statistics for fertilizer sales and average prices in the year 1880, and presented calculations to show that a difference of 1% in the analysis for reduced phosphoric acid made a difference of $50,000 in the annual production of a "good-sized factory." The monetary loss was only one part of the problem, since there were also the possible loss of business, loss of reputation, law suits, and condemnation of the product by state officials. He felt that the convention agreements could not really solve the complex problems of methodology, and that the tendency to revert, after the convention, to methods which had been in use for many years in any individual laboratory was too strong to overcome that way.

As a solution to the difficulties, he pointed out that most of the states had departments of agriculture and each such department had at least one eminent chemist assigned to the analysis of commercial fertilizers. These chemists had no reason to be biased with regard to the analytical results obtained, and were furnished, generally, with well equipped laboratories, competent assistants, and resources provided by the fertilizer taxes. Shephard suggested that a very satisfactory arrangement would require that the relatively small number of official chemists agree on methods and that the commercial chemists would then be compelled to use them. He cautioned the official chemists with the "earnest advice to agree upon no method of analysis before thoroughly testing it by repeated actual investigations on the part of all official laboratories, and to refrain from adopting it until concordant results are secured from all participants." Shephard felt that the commercial chemist should participate in the testing programs, but that initiation and conduct of the studies should be handled by the official chemists. Dr. Shephard also proposed that during the convention only state chemists and chemists from boards of agriculture and experiment stations be allowed to vote on questions of methods for fertilizer analysis. Such proposals were adopted in principle by the new organization later, but the convention delegates decided at this time to keep the voting procedure as it had been. All enrolled members retained their voting rights.

Most of the first day of the meeting was concerned with discussions of the various forms of phosphoric acid, and efforts to define terms, such as "reverted," reduced, and precipitated phosphoric acid. During these discussions, Dr. Wiley described his innovative use of the Gooch crucible in phosphoric acid determinations and concluded, "One who has not used this method can scarcely realize the advantage it possesses over all others." In an age of electronic instrumentation and computers, it is interesting to recall that such simple devices have advanced analytical chemistry.

During the second day there were reports, presentations of analytical data, and discussions of methods for determination of nitrogen and potash. The methods adopted by the convention were printed in the bulletin containing the proceedings. There was also discussion of the propriety of assigning commercial values to fertilizers. A proposed "American Journal of Agricultural Science" was described to the meeting and won the convention endorsement and pledges of support from its members, but the journal apparently was never published.

Before the convention adjourned, a committee was appointed to "consider plans and take steps looking at the permanent organization of this body of agricultural chemists." The committee was asked to report at the next meeting to be held in conjunction with the meeting of AAAS in Philadelphia, Pennsylvania, during September 4-10, 1884.

The Philadelphia meeting, which was to become the first meeting of the Association of Official Agricultural Chemists, began on September 8, 1884. Again, the state chemists were prominent in the list of attendees. The committee that had been appointed at the Atlanta meeting to consider the question of organizing as a subsection of AAAS submitted a report recommending the formation of two organizations: an Association of Official Agricultural Chemists, to make decisions as to methods of analysis, etc., having no connection with AAAS; and a subsection of AAAS, which would be open to all agricultural chemists for the purposes of investigation and discussion. After the report was discussed, it was unanimously decided that any union with AAAS was not desirable and the formation of an entirely separate organization was the best method of advancing the objectives of the convention. A committee was immediately appointed to decide on a recommended form of organization and to report on the next day, September 9.

The report of the committee was submitted in the form of the "Constitution of the Association of Official Agricultural Chemists." The objectives were "to secure, as far as possible, uniformity in legislation with regard to the regulations of the sale of commercial fertilizers in the different states and uniformity and accuracy in the methods and results of fertilizer analysis." Membership was declared open to "analytical chemists connected with state departments of agriculture, state experiment stations, and state boards, exercising an official fertilizer control." One representative from each institution was to be entitled to a vote when properly accredited. It was further allowed that "all analytical chemists and others interested in the objectives of the Association may attend its meetings and take part in its discussions, but shall have no vote in the Association." An Executive Committee was specified to consist of the President, Vice President, and Secretary, who also served as Treasurer, along with two other elected members.

This committee was empowered to further define the duties of the officers of the Association when necessary and to call special meetings. It was also given the responsibility to confer with the official boards represented as to the payment of meeting expenses and publication of the proceedings of the Association. Three standing committees of three members each were designated for phosphoric acid, potash, and nitrogen, respectively. Their duties were "to test methods, to distribute samples to members of the Association and others who may signify their desire to participate in the work, and to present a written report at each annual meeting embodying the progress made during the year in analytical methods bearing on their respective topics and the results of work done under their direction."

The date for the annual meeting was also set in the Constitution as the first Tuesday in September.

During the discussion of the proposed Constitution, the only real question concerned the provision on participation, which excluded unofficial or commercial chemists from membership. Since the fertilizer manufacturers had no objection to the stated arrangement, the new Constitution was unanimously adopted, formal organization took place, and the first annual meeting of AOAC was held. Professor S.W. Johnson of Connecticut was elected the first president of the new organization for the following year. Since Dr. Johnson was not present, Professor H.C. White of Georgia, the vice president, chaired the meeting, which adopted several methods for phosphorus and potash for the next season. The proceedings of this meeting, including the Constitution and methods adopted, comprised only eight pages.

The Early Years of Growth

While the individual state experiment stations and agricultural colleges and state departments of agriculture were lending their support to the new Association and its objectives, the United States Commissioner of Agriculture, the Hon. Norman J. Colman, was also very generous. He approved the active participation of his Chief of the Bureau of Chemistry, Dr. Harvey Wiley, and others on his staff, and also provided facilities in the department buildings for the annual meeting for many years. He also established the precedent of printing the proceedings and the recommended methods as part of the Bulletin Series of the Division of Chemistry (later Bureau of Chemistry), which continued until Wiley's departure from the Bureau in 1912.

The second annual meeting of the Association was held in the USDA library, with Professor H.C. White of Georgia presiding in Professor Johnson's absence. Commissioner Colman addressed the meeting, and, after affirming his approval of the goals proposed, he expressed the hope that the work of the Association would not be limited to obtaining uniform methods for fertilizer analysis, but that it would be expanded to include chemical analysis in general. He drew attention to the need in particular for standards of purity of foods and methods of detecting adulteration. In his letter of invitation for the third convention to be held at the USDA facilities, Colman again expressed his hopes that the Association would extend its activities to other areas in addition to fertilizer analyses. Dr. Wiley, the new president, addressed the Association at the opening of the third convention, setting a precedent for a presidential address at each convention, which has been broken very infrequently over almost 100 years. Wiley closed his address with a reiteration of the proposal that the Association extend its investigations over a wider range of subjects. He suggested that any problem in chemical agricultural analysis was proper for discussion at the meetings, and proposed that a committee be appointed to consider the propriety of revising the part of the Constitution which limited the scope of the investigations and the membership. Reports were presented on phosphoric acid, potash, and nitrogen, but no official method could yet be agreed on for nitrogen. At this meeting, the recommended expansion of AOAC interests and subjects for study was begun with the appointment of two additional commodity committees: one for animal foodstuffs and one for dairy products.

Reports on both cattle food and dairy products were delivered at the fourth annual meeting along with the usual three major fertilizer element reports. At this meeting, two more subjects were adopted for study with appointment of committees on analysis of fermented liquors and analysis for fermented sugars. At the urging of the President, Dr. E.H. Jenkins of the Connecticut Experiment

Station, an amendment to the Constitution was adopted to clarify that chemists from agricultural colleges who exercised no official control over the materials connected with the agricultural industry, and also chemists from U.S. government agencies (such as the Treasury Department) were eligible for membership. The question of sampling procedures for fertilizers was raised at this meeting by Mr. A. DeGhequier, the Secretary of the National Fertilizer Association, who participated in most of the early meetings. He pointed out that in many cases only a single bag was being sampled; he recommended that chemists agree on a representative number of sacks and that samples be drawn from various portions of the sack, not just the top, as was often the practice. He asked that duplicate samples be taken so that the manufacturer could obtain one on request if a question arose concerning the analytical results. This philosophy that the "analysis is only as good as the sample" is still a basic tenet of agricultural analytical chemistry and AOAC has done a great deal of valuable work over the years on the subject of sampling to assure uniformity.

Other changes in organizational structure of the Association and in methods of operation took place during the early years as interests and activities expanded and membership increased. At the fifth meeting in 1888, a constitutional amendment was adopted to put the responsibility for each subject in the hands of one person, called a reporter, instead of a committee of three as had been done until then. This designation was changed to "Referee" in 1897. By this time, the objectives had been expanded to include the securing of "uniformity and accuracy in the methods, results, and modes of statements of analysis of fertilizers, soils, cattle foods, dairy products, and other materials connected with agricultural industry."

At the sixth meeting, Harvey W. Wiley began his long tenure as Secretary of the Association, a position he occupied for over 20 years, again setting a precedent, this time for continuity in management of AOAC through extended tenure of the Secretary. It was that same year that USDA, which supplied resources and support for the Association, became an executive department of the U.S. government, emphasizing the growing national recognition of scientific agriculture. The close liaison was sustained by mutual interests and also through the efforts of Dr. Wiley and the Hon. Edwin Willits, the Assistant Secretary of Agriculture, who addressed many of the early meetings.

By this time, every fertilizer-producing state in the country recognized by special enactment the methods of fertilizer analysis adopted by AOAC. As President John Meyers expressed the situation in 1889, AOAC was "aiming to lay a foundation so solid that every court in this land must respect its conclusions, and every analytical chemist, whether living in this country or elsewhere, must be forced either to practice or admit the advantages and correctness of our system of analyses. Step by step we have advanced through the difficult problems before us, feeling that we have steadily gained ground and that we are molding public sentiment in a manner that must redound to the advantage of the whole country and secure the highest respect for the science to which we are devoting our lives. We have, in five years, developed, under the pressure to which we have been subjected, an association which is recognized by one of the most progressive governments of the world as being reliable, its conclusions are very largely accepted in the courts of the country and adopted as trustworthy by a number of our state legislatures." Meyers pointed out that there were then 46 state experiment stations, each employing at least one analyst, giving the country a body of scientists engaged in agricultural analyses which in numbers, he felt, compared well with the agricultural chemists in the whole of Europe. The success of AOAC was bound to be enhanced by this involvement.

One consideration of major importance was the conduct of collaborative studies of methods. There was the question of whether such samples were testing the methodology or the analyst. A study in 1889 of the analysis of uniform samples sent out by the Association had shown that results depended a great deal more on the individual skill of each analyst and on attention to seemingly unimportant details of the method than had been realized. The premise was generally accepted that, since the testing of methods and their official adoption was the prime objective, it was improper to deviate in any way from the prescribed method, and that competent, experienced analysts should be assigned the task of analyzing the test samples. It was considered inappropriate to use this procedure to evaluate the abilities of inexperienced analysts or assistants.

During the meeting of the Association of Agricultural Colleges and Experiment Stations in 1889, the methods of AOAC were further recognized when it was resolved that all analyses at experiment stations be done by methods adopted by AOAC, and that if any chemists saw reasons for following other methods, these reasons should be stated with the published results. This step enormously increased the amount of work which would be done according to AOAC methods and made the task of critically evaluating each method even more compelling.

Another problem concerning the Association was uniformity of fertilizer laws. The original constitution had stated as an objective "to secure as far as possible uniformity of legislation," but the committee appointed in 1885 for that purpose never reported. In 1886, the National Fertilizer Association, interested in abolishing commercial valuation of fertilizers, urged AOAC to cooperate in influencing the passage of national fertilizer legislation, but the members did not want to go beyond individual state responsibilities. The clause on uniformity of legislation was eliminated from the Constitution in 1886, which left the delegates free to discuss it without taking a positive stance. Labeling was also a major problem, since a manufacturer might need 10 or more different labels for doing business in that many states. The feeling in the organization as expressed by E.B. Voorhes, Director of the New Jersey Agricultural Experiment Station, in his presidential address in 1894, was that "We are an association of agricultural chemists, not mere analysts, and are, or should be, interested in the far reaching influence of a proper chemical analysis."

The vulnerability of some of the methodology was indicated by Dr. S.M. Babcock in his presidential address of 1893 when he suggested that, while most of the AOAC methods were well adapted to determine the value of the agricultural constituents they measured, the analysis of fodder provided a notable exception. He noted that dried excrement, analyzed in digestion experiments, often gave figures corresponding almost exactly with those from the best feed; also, that a mixture of the proper proportions of such substances as leather scraps, sawdust, oxalic acid, and kerosene could give results which correspond with those from any fodder. He strongly suggested that a system dealing with the proximate constituents of fodders be adopted. His scheme was not adopted, since it entailed considerably more time and labor than was considered practical. Much work was done on developing specific methods, however, and microscopic examination eventually eliminated some of the possibilities of gross adulteration.

When the tenth annual convention in 1893 was held in Chicago during the Columbian Exhibition, AOAC worked in conjunction with the American Chemical Society (ACS) and AAAS in a successful effort to secure an international congress of chemists to coincide with the meetings. Partly as a result of the beneficial contact with foreign scientists at that meeting, it was proposed that the Executive Committee take such steps as it might deem expedient to bring about more general international cooperation in the study of methods of analysis. In carrying out this first attempt at international cooperation, Dr. Wiley wrote to over 250 foreign chemists, inviting their participation in the work of AOAC. This was the beginning of cooperation with foreign chemists, foreign organizations, and international groups for the establishment of uniform methods, standards, and regulations which, as we shall see, has become a major function of the Association. At the World Congress of Applied Chemistry in Paris, 1895, action was taken to publish the AOAC methods in French and German under the sanction of the Congress. This made European chemists much more familiar with them.

The organization continued to flourish with no major changes. At the eleventh meeting in 1894, a communication was read from the Society of Leather Chemists requesting that they be incorporated into the organization and that a reporter for tannin be appointed. This was approved on motion, and a reporter was appointed.

Associate reporters were authorized, at that time, by amendment to the Constitution. Their duties were not defined, but it was understood that they should prepare to take the place of reporters.

In 1895, President H.A. Huston, the State Chemist of Indiana, noted a problem which had been receiving much attention, but on which AOAC had taken little action: the composition and analysis of human food. He stated that "while our reports abound in researches on food for livestock, the only work on human food is represented in the reports on dairy products and sugar, and as a rule, comparatively few of us contribute to either of these branches. Even the question of hotel accommodations was referred to the committee on fermented and distilled liquors." He cited the fact that the Constitution was revised in 1885 to permit membership of municipal chemists, whose duties included inspection of many articles of human food. He cited the valuable work on human food being done in the Division of Chemistry of USDA and suggested that AOAC should become active in this field, especially in support of the municipal chemist.

Food for Thought

The subject of possible AOAC involvement in pure food legislation and food analysis methodology was being brought to the attention of the conventions continuously and was the subject of much discussion at the meetings. In the 1895 meeting, a committee was organized to consider in what way the Association could be of service in formulating a pure food law. The committee consisted of H.W. Wiley, H.A. Huston, J.A. Myers, and A.S. Mitchell; a report was given the following year.

William Frear, addressing the convention in his capacity as president in 1897, again broached the subject of human food and of detection of adulteration. He pointed out that the limited number of food methods, studied by AOAC for milk and sugar products and alcoholic liquors, did not confront the serious problem of adulteration. Efforts had been directed primarily toward perfection of methods intended to determine the normal constituents of these food materials. Frear maintained that this should continue, but argued that detection of adulteration should be pursued also, and presented detailed statistics to illustrate the enormous economic importance of processed foods subject to possible adulteration. He suggested two ways the Association could aid the food control chemist. First, he maintained, food control chemists differed in their results of analysis of the same products because of the differences in methods used. The situation was much the same as the fertilizer chemists faced when the Association was first organized. He referred to the recent appointment of a referee on food adulteration and felt that the Association was on its way to making major progress in establishing uniformity for methods to detect adulteration. The second way he suggested to aid the food control chemist was to help secure the establishment of standards of composition for pure food substances in much the same way pharmacists had done for drugs. He cited the example of the *United States Pharmacopeia* as the accepted authority on standards of purity for drugs and even a few food substances under most state and municipal laws. The food chemist needed a similar set of standards, since the practice of the time was to adopt arbitrary standards which varied among different chemists and had no legal standing. Such arbitrary standards not based on reliable facts of food composition could produce unfair hardships for both sides. The problems of impure, decomposed, and adulterated foods and of fraudulent and dangerous drugs and patent medicines were not new. AOAC was urgently requested to consider these problems in its methods program. A host of early instances of alleged adulteration, some true and many false, are recounted in Frederick A. Filby's *A History of Adulteration*. This book cites examples of such crimes as early as the fourteenth century in England. Some early examples of adulterated foods included pepper containing gravel, leaves, twigs, stalks, cochineal dye, or even poisonous red lead, and sugar adulterated with sand, dust, lime, pulp, or coloring matter. Essential oils were diluted with less expensive liquids such as oil of turpentine. Tea was another grocery item easily subject to adulteration both by mixing with other leaves and by deceptive coloring. Early adulterations of bread, beer, wines, and liquors are also cited. Many of these transgressions were still prevalent in the late 1800s in the United States, along with new ones, such as adulteration of butter with margarine.

According to Filby, the turning point which aroused general public recognition, interest, and indignation regarding impurities in foods was the publication by an Englishman, Frederick Accum, of *A Treatise on Adulteration of Food and Culinary Poisons*. He exhibited the fraudulent adulterations of bread, beer, wine, and other articles employed in domestic economy in 1820, and reported methods of detecting such fraud. From that time on, there was increased public awareness of the problem. Another important English figure in the early detection of fraud in foods was Arthur Hill Hassel. His fame rests primarily upon his introduction of the microscope into food analysis, with which he and his students discovered many previously undetected cases of adulteration. They produced a complete set of diagrams illustrating various pure and adulterated foodstuffs under both medium and high power magnification. Hassel also used the existing chemical knowledge in his inspection of suspect foods. After 1820, when methods were available for detection of many of the undeclared ingredients, numerous such additives were found. Pepper continued to be highly adulterated; among the items found in it were linseed meal, wheat flour, mustard husks, rice flour, pepper dust, and gypsum. Lime was added to ginger to protect it from insects, and fumes from burning sulfur were used to improve its appearance. Ginger was also diluted with tapioca, potato flour, ground rice, turmeric, and other foreign materials; these became apparent under Hassel's microscope. Vinegar was diluted with sulfuric acid in more cases than not. Most pickles contained traces of copper, and metallic poisons were also found in jellies and cheese. Butter was diluted with potato flour and as much as 50% oleomargarine after its introduction about 1880. Most of these problems and many more were documented in England and in the United States food supply.

Several investigations, prompted by publication of the chemical and microscopic analyses, resulted in the passage in England of the Adulteration of Food Act of 1860. This law empowered local authorities to appoint competent analysts and provided for fines for those selling adulterated articles. Since this act did not require the appointment of analysts, it had little impact on the situation. In 1872, a new act was passed providing for the compulsory

Bureau of Chemistry microchemistry laboratory.

appointment of analysts and inspectors. It also provided more severe penalties. Shortly after the passage of this act, the Society of Public Analysts was formed. This auspicious group of chemists, analysts, and doctors soon drew up a workable general definition of adulteration and gave real effectiveness to the law.

Progress in the United States was not so rapid. However, there was growing concern over the food supply, as we have noted from the increasing pressure on AOAC to involve itself more heavily in food analysis methods. The first step in food control had been taken in 1850 with the passage of the law regulating classification of tea, but the problem of adulteration had not been seriously considered. Although some problems undoubtedly existed, they were minor, considering the fact that until the last two or three decades of the nineteenth century the majority of our population raised most of what they consumed and their medication consisted of standard, proven remedies. After the Civil War, however, the surge in industrial growth in the United States created many changes in life styles, including the way we obtained our food. During the 1880s, the food supply system underwent a period of revolution as the population rapidly became more urbanized. Citizens increasingly demanded a supply of preserved and canned food. In this burgeoning food products industry, entrepreneurs abounded. Many turned to the cheapest and easiest methods of preserving their products, with the natural consequence that many of the finished products were adulterated or misbranded. Many of the preservatives used were recognized as toxic. At this same time, a substantial surge in activity occurred as medicine manufacturers began selling their nostrums and remedies through advertising. They used false, misleading, or wildly exaggerated claims in many instances. The public apathy was bemoaned by Harvey Wiley, who later recounted in his autobiography: "Most of the panacea vendors were amazed at the results they had hoped for but hardly dared anticipate. Every citizen, male or female, married or single, young or old, was a potential customer for every 'cure' placed on the market, for every one either had something the matter with him or feared he might have, and whatever the ill might be the nostrum was guaranteed to cure it. The newspapers of 1883 carried few news illustrations, but plenty of ridiculous 'before and after taking' pictures."

Wiley and the Food and Drug Act

It was in this crucial period that Dr. Harvey Wiley began his campaign for a law to provide protection for the consumer against adulterated and misbranded food and medicines. A copious quantity of literature has been written by and about this remarkable man, who is still referred to as the "Father of the Pure Food and Drug Law." It is appropriate at this point to briefly review his life as well as his activities leading up to the passage of the first U.S. Federal Food and Drug Act in 1906.

Harvey Washington Wiley was born on a farm near the village of Kent, Indiana, in 1844; he enrolled in nearby Hanover College at the age of 19 in 1863. He left college briefly in 1864 to fight in the Civil War and then resumed his studies at Hanover, graduating in June of 1867. He then taught public school before beginning studies for his medical degree at Indiana Medical College. While attending this institution, he earned his living as an instructor of Latin and Greek at Northwestern Christian University (which became Butler University).

Wiley received his medical degree in 1871 and accepted a position as science teacher in the Central High School in Indianapolis. A year later he was offered the chair of chemistry at Indiana Medical School, which he accepted with the provision that he could take a course of advanced study before assuming his duties. He felt that he was not sufficiently advanced in chemistry yet to occupy such an important post. He traveled to Cambridge, Massachusetts, for the next phase of his education at Harvard, where he was privileged to attend lectures by Louis Agassis and John Tyndall, as well as the distinguished faculty of that chemistry department, including Charles E. Munroe.

After a residency of about five months, and after passing oral and written examinations for entry into the freshmen, sophomore, and junior classes and also working off two senior conditions in a total of 17 days, Wiley was awarded his Bachelor of Science degree (cum laude) from Harvard. He referred to himself as "perhaps the most rapidly catapulted graduate the Lawrence School ever had." Wiley was adopted into the Harvard class of 1873 even though he had been a special student at the Lawrence Scientific School.

Returning to Indiana, the industrious Wiley assumed the chair in chemisty at the Indiana Medical College. He arranged his schedule so that he could also accept the chair in chemistry at Northwestern Christian University, teaching all his classes there in the morning. He decided to postpone his practice of medicine for a year. Perhaps this left him with too much time on his hands, because he then accepted the position of physiology teacher in the city high school, in addition to his other duties, when the regular teacher fell ill. This schedule began early each morning and continued until 10 o'clock each night. In his autobiography, Wiley declares of this period: "Every day was a joy, and with three salaries I considered that I was on the road to early wealth. My combined income for the year amounted to over fourteen hundred dollars." Unfortunately, Wiley contracted meningitis and almost died before this busy academic year ended.

Before the new term began the following year, he was offered and accepted the position as the first professor of chemistry and youngest member of the teaching staff at Purdue University at Lafayette, Indiana, which was just about to open for the first time. He became State Chemist of Indiana by virtue of this appointment and also retained his position at the Medical College, but did relinquish all other positions. Wiley had many interesting exploits at the new institution, where he volunteered also to teach military tactics, drawing on his army experience.

In 1878, he took a leave of absence from Purdue for a semester to travel to Europe, where he visited with many of the prominent chemists of the time. He was inspired to examine food products by some of his observations in European health laboratories, and, on returning to Lafayette, he secured permission from the Indiana State Board of Health to examine sugars and syrups for adulteration. This was the beginning of his activities in the interest of pure foods, which was to become the passion and focus of the rest of his life.

Although he was later seriously considered for the position of President of Purdue, he did also encounter problems, often with a humorous twist. One of the most famous stories, which he relates in his autobiography and which has been frequently retold, concerns his free spirit and the repercussions it caused. Wiley had bought a nickel-plated Harvard roadster bicycle with a high front wheel and a small back wheel, which did not find favor among some on campus. Wiley's ecstatic description states: "Sitting on this vehicle made one feel as if one were riding through thin air. Striking a stone or stump meant disaster, for undignified fall was the result. I acquired a bicycle uniform with knee breeches, and I rode daily through the streets of Lafayette, over the bridge across the Wabash and up to the University, frightening horses, attracting attention and grieving the hearts of staid presidents and professors, as well as members of the board of trustees." Wiley was subsequently called before a session of the Board of Trustees, at which time, instead of the salary increase he expected, he was given generous praise for

Harvey Wiley (third from right) and his staff, about 1883.

his excellence of instruction and popularity with the students and then reprimanded for his conduct. The two complaints were that he had put on a uniform and played baseball with the boys, and that he had bought a bicycle and was observed "dressed up like a monkey and astride a cartwheel riding along our streets." Wiley countered by resigning his position, and the resignation was promptly rejected. The bicycle wound up in the Purdue museum and, with typical Wiley humor, the cyclist wrote in his autobiography, "I fear the fact that I started the first chemical laboratories at Purdue and presided over them for nine years will gradually fade from the memory of man. I feel inclined to pin my hopes of immortality at Purdue to the old bicycle in the museum."

In 1883, Wiley left Purdue to accept the position of chief of the Division of Chemistry of USDA in Washington, in which he served for 29 years. Dr. Collier, his predecessor, had been working on the idea of the use of sorghum as a domestic sugar source. Wiley continued this program and expanded it immensely with great success during his tenure in the Department of Agriculture. The chemists in the department had been interested in the study of food and drug adulteration for several years. With the arrival of the new chief chemist, this work was raised to the highest priority and continued until the successful enactment of the Food and Drug Act in 1906.

Wiley and his coworkers extensively studied the use of preservatives in canned meat and in canned vegetables; they reported their findings on such chemicals as potassium nitrate, sulfuric acid, benzoic acid, salicylic acid, boric acid, salt, saccharin, and hydronaphthol in the bulletins of USDA, Bureau of Chemistry. Wiley was generally opposed to the use of added preservatives, but he did recognize that absolute prohibition was not necessarily warranted in some instances. He did, however, insist that when any use of a preservative was deemed to be warranted, it should be declared on the label.

With the steadily increasing interest in purity of foods and the nature and safety of preservatives and other additives, Wiley requested special funds for experiments. By a special act of Congress he obtained authority to set up the experiment which became famous as Wiley's Poison Squad. The purpose of the act as stated was: "To enable the Secretary of Agriculture to investigate the character of food preservatives, coloring matters and other substances added to foods to determine their relation to digestion and health, and to establish the principles which should guide their use." Wiley conducted feeding studies using human volunteers, young men who were employees of the Department of Agriculture. He first standardized each group by establishing a diet which maintained constant weight in each subject. Then the adulterated food was fed, and weight loss or other deleterious clinical effects were observed and measured. Feces and urine were analyzed and results were tabulated.

Dr. Wiley personally supervised these experiments in which the men ate and drank nothing except the experimental diet items while participating in tests. During the five years over which the tests were conducted, the various meals contained boric acid and borax, salicylic acid and salicylates, sulfurous acid and sulfites, benzoic acid and benzoates, formaldehyde, copper sulfate, and saltpeter. The findings were published as parts of Bulletin 84 of the Bureau of Chemistry and supported the contention that those commonly used preservatives were indeed injurious to health.

As previously mentioned, the first law passed in the United States aimed at providing a purer food supply was passed in 1850. It regulated the classification of tea and it prohibited the importation of teas which did not conform to the types required. The first drug statute passed, the Import Drug Act of 1848, provided for laboratory inspection at ports of entry; it resulted from publicity given to the report that American troops in Mexico had been supplied with adulterated quinine. The first bona fide pure food bill was supported by AOAC. It was introduced in the Senate in 1889 by Senator A.S. Paddock of Nebraska, and was passed, only to be rejected in the House. Several similar bills were introduced in succeeding sessions; while they usually passed in the House or Senate, they could not muster enough support to to be successful in both houses. Such bills were frequently treated with ridicule or frivolity and were considered to be the handiwork of cranks. In spite of this, the general interest in a pure food law was growing, and the leaders in Congress were gradually beginning to recognize the serious problems which existed.

A great deal of lobbying was being done by vested interests: the manufacturers who used chemical preservatives, manufacturers of the adulterants, compounders of imitation whisky, purveyors of worthless patent medicines, and those manufacturers and merchants who were generally misbranding and mislabeling foods and drugs. The Bureau of Chemistry collected a plethora of false advertising replete with impossible claims and promises to cure all possible ills. The products were found to be, in the case of most of the so-called tonics and elixirs, only alcoholic drinks. Many of the patent medicines, frequently recommended for incurable diseases, were worthless or even poisonous. The enormous amount of money being spent on advertising in newspapers and magazines was an additional obstacle, since only the most honest and responsible publishers or editors would refuse such largesse. One such editor was Edward Bok of *The Ladies Home Journal*, who published

THE "POISON SQUAD," AN INTERESTING AND UNIQUE ORGANIZATION OF TWELVE VOLUNTEERS

THESE YOUNG MEN ARE EXPERIMENTED UPON BY THE UNITED STATES BUREAU OF CHEMISTRY

MR. B. J. HOWARD AND HIS MARVELOUS PHOTO-MICROGRAPHIC APPARATUS

Top: The "poison squad." Bottom: B.J. Howard and his photomicrographic apparatus.

exposés of the fraudulent products and did much to make the public aware of the mounting problem. William Allen White of the Kansas Emporia Gazette took the lead in refusing fraudulent advertising.

During this period, AOAC and its members were actively supporting the struggle for national as well as state legislation. In his AOAC presidential address in 1900, B.W. Kilgore announced that he had "used the name of the Association and joined other scientific bodies in this country in asking the Congress to pass a national food law."

Dr. Harvey Wiley had a major role in writing the historic bill which bore the name of Senator W.S. Heyburn of Ohio. This bill, in spite of frantic lobbying efforts and open attacks by opponents, finally passed both Houses of Congress on June 30, 1906, and was signed by President Theodore Roosevelt on the same day. It had taken almost 25 years to achieve the victory. State governments were stimulated to revise their legislation as a result of the new act.

The new law prohibited the interstate sale of adulterated foods, beverages, and drugs, and placed the authority for enforcement in the Bureau of Chemistry, headed by Wiley, who has become generally acknowledged as the "Father of the Pure Food Law."

A committee representing the Secretary of Commerce and Labor, the Secretary of the Treasury, and the Secretary of Agriculture formulated rules and regulations for enforcement. The struggle for pure foods was by no means over and Wiley met with heartbreaking frustrations in his efforts to administer the new law as he interpreted it, but the country was finally on the way toward that goal.

Fortunately, the labors of the enforcement officers were abetted by the efforts of the Food Standards Committee. The Congress had mandated this committee through the 1902 appropriations bill for the Department of Agriculture and authorized the Secretary of Agriculture to appoint such a committee. Since the detection of fraud, adulteration, and mislabeling depended on comparison with a standard of purity or measure, AOAC had a great interest in standards. The standards movement in the United States was strongly supported by AOAC, which appointed a standing committee on volumetric standards in 1896 and a committee for the uniform statement of results of fertilizer analysis in 1897. In 1900, the Association supported the bill in Congress for the "National Standardizing Bureau," which became the National Bureau of Standards. The AOAC Food Standards Committee began its work in 1897, and AOAC delegates were also appointed to the Pure Food

Convention. In 1902, Congress officially recognized the Association by making it advisor to the Secretary of Agriculture in all matters relating to food standards. The Joint Committee on Standards formed by the Secretary of Agriculture at that time included outstanding representatives of various agricultural experiment stations and agricultural colleges. Four of the five original members had been presidents of AOAC. The standards promulgated by this esteemed committee became the guide for the enforcement of the National Food Law and were also adopted by many states.

Soon after the Food and Drug Act went into effect on January 1, 1907, a series of frustrating experiences began which plagued Wiley until his resignation in 1912. Although most food manufacturers and dealers were quite willing to operate within the constraints of the law, several notable groups felt that their businesses would be ruined if they were obliged to observe the statute. Among these were manufacturers who were using sulfur dioxide as a bleach in sugar processing and those who used it as a preservative for dried fruit. Whisky "rectifers," patent medicine makers, manufacturers of alum baking powers, and those using saccharin and caffeine in their products also challenged the law.

Wiley fought hard in every case, but was generally ineffective because the administrative establishment yielded to pressures from industry and political groups that could not coerce Wiley directly. This was accomplished by two boards which were intended to usurp his authority. The first of these was the Board of Food and Drug Inspection, on which Secretary of Agriculture Wilson placed Wiley along with two other members whom the Secretary knew would maintain a majority to overrule Wiley's decisions. The second was the Board of Consulting Scientific Experts appointed by President Roosevelt and chaired by Ira Remsen, who was recognized as the discoverer of saccharin. Wiley found himself continually at odds with these groups, since they maintained positions far more liberal than his on the toxicity of many additives.

Wiley felt that most of the "rights and privileges" which the law had given the Bureau of Chemistry had been delegated to the board and that "The Pure Food and Drug Act was virtually repealed by executive edict." Nevertheless, he continued to battle the foes of the Pure Food and Drug Act in the Bureau of Chemistry until 1912, when he resigned. During this period he continued the Bureau's investigations on possible harmful substances in foods. His findings showed that many coal tar dyes were toxic. He established a policy of certification of the dyes which were found acceptable. Each batch was examined by a Bureau of Chemistry chemist and given a certification number.

Harvey Wiley and his staff, about 1900.

Bureau of Chemistry Food Standards Committee, about 1900. Wiley is second from right.

Shortly before Wiley's resignation, he was accused and then exonerated of the charge of improper practices in hiring a consultant medical doctor at a fee higher than the one designated in the government salary scale for per diem employees. Although he was completely vindicated, and the report of the investigating committee condemned the referee board and the Department of Agriculture administration for hampering the proper enforcement of the Pure Food and Drug Act, Wiley felt that he should retire from his position. He had married in 1911 at the age of 66 and desired to spend more time with his young family. He no longer wanted to fight the antagonism of Secretary Wilson and his associates on the Board of Food and Drug Inspection, but he did not have a defeated outlook in spite of his adversities. As he put it in his autobiography, "On the other hand I knew that I had completed a great work in the Pure Food and Drug Act and that I had carried on its enforcement during its first six years of existence to the satisfaction of the people whom it was intended to protect. The press was now almost unanimously and vociferously behind me. I felt an intense satisfaction in the realization that I had won, under countless handicaps and against terrific opposition, all the big battles I had been in for the public welfare." The Bureau had grown from six employees to over 600 during Wiley's tenure from 1883 to 1912, and many new laboratories and food inspection stations had been established. Wiley accepted the position of director of the Bureau of Foods, Sanitation, and Health in the editorial department of *Good Housekeeping Magazine* and spent the next 17 years continuing his crusade for pure foods and drugs and good health from that forum.

Reports of the meetings of the Association and the publication of AOAC official methods, as they appeared in the bulletins of the Bureau of Chemistry, were always introduced by a letter of transmittal from the chief of the bureau. Each of these was signed by Harvey W. Wiley until the twenty-ninth annual convention in 1912 when Wiley resigned from the Bureau, and the letter of transmittal to Secretary of Agriculture Wilson bore the signature of Carl L. Alsberg, the new chief of the Bureau of Chemistry, who became Secretary of AOAC the following year. At the same time, Wiley became ineligible for active membership in AOAC since he was no longer a control official or official chemist. The Association reacted by making Wiley not only an honorary life member but also honorary president. Wiley attended meetings and participated in AOAC activities until his death, and was the recipient of many honors from AOAC, the American Chemical Society (ACS), and other organizations as well as governments. He delivered an extemporaneous address at each annual meeting on a wide variety of scientific subjects, always with good humor and calling attention to the practical scientific problems of the times. In 1908, ACS held a testimonial banquet in Wiley's honor to celebrate his twenty-fifth anniversary in the service of the Department of

Harvey Wiley in his laboratory, about 1910.

Agriculture. Wiley had been extremely active in ACS, had been a leader in its early reorganization and expansion, and had served as its president in 1893 and 1894.

In 1924, on his eightieth birthday, AOAC honored Dr. Wiley with a banquet. The humorous menu for this occasion was a reminder of Wiley's many struggles in behalf of pure foods. It listed such items as arsenical celery, botulism olives, borated baked bluefish, renovated cream butter, and Wiley rooster, well stuffed and roasted. A bronze plaque was presented to him at the dinner. It bore a bas-relief portrait of Wiley and the inscription on the reverse side: "Presented to Harvey W. Wiley on his eightieth birthday, Oct. 18, 1924, at the fortieth anniversary of the Association of Official Agricultural Chemists, in recognition of his service to chemistry, agriculture, hygiene and public welfare." Small replicas of the medal were given to the dinner guests, and the die has been used for producing more such replicas on more recent occasions. A reproduction of it is embedded in Wiley's gravestone in Arlington Cemetery. Wiley's memory has been observed over the many years since his death by various annual awards bearing his name. These will be discussed later. He has also been nominated for the Hall of Fame on three occasions.

For one transitional year, W.D. Bigelow, Wiley's assistant for many years in the Bureau of Foods, acted as Secretary of AOAC. Then from 1914 through 1920, Carl Alsberg very ably handled the affairs of the organization, acting as his predecessors had in the capacity of Treasurer as well as Secretary.

AOAC continued in the forefront of the struggle for food protection. It had consistently urged the passage of regulatory legislation and supported the realistic attainment of regulatory goals by participating in the development of definitions of standards, as well as by developing proven standard methods. At the same time, the young organization was occupied with refining its goals and objectives and further establishing its identity in terms of eligibility for membership. These have never been static in the 100 years of existence of AOAC and are even now in a healthy state of change to meet the challenges of political, social, industrial, and technological changes and advances.

From its very inception, the Association began to enlarge its scope of activities to gradually encompass more of the commodities which fell under the possible scrutiny of the official or agricultural chemists in the various states and federal government. Each remains an ongoing concern. At the twentieth annual convention in 1903, President R. J. Davidson again addressed the question of uniform laws for commercial fertilizers. In his examination of 23 state laws, he found no mutual agreement, either as to requirements

AOAC meeting in Washington, DC, November 1908.

or as to the form in which the composition was to be stated. He urged that AOAC exert its influence to make these laws conform to some definite standard representing plain, simple, understandable statements in regard to the constituents. He urged the adoption by all states of the AOAC fertilizer standards which had been prepared by the committee on Uniform Fertilizer Legislation, adopted by AOAC five years previously, and subsequently adopted by the American Association of Agricultural Colleges and Experiment Stations. Davidson suggested that the Association adopt a uniform method of reporting results on all the subjects it had under consideration.

In 1907, President J. P. Street expressed his satisfaction that the collaborative work was again being performed by experienced analysts. However, the question of methods being rejected because of the use of inexperienced analysts had continued to plague the organization. A.L. Winton had complained about the problem in 1898 and A.H. Wheeler in his presidential address the following year. The problem has turned out to be a perennial one. There is still a need to confirm the analyst's skill in order to ascertain the reliability of a method under collaborative study.

A major procedural change occurred as a result of Professor Street's recommendation that a permanent committee on methods be established to minimize the problem of maintaining continuity while the volunteer cooperators were continually changing. This committee was composed of three subcommittees of three members each which received all annual reports at least three weeks before the meeting, allowing time for reports to be edited and reviewed for presentation. The adopted methods could then be incorporated into the official methods publication in an orderly fashion. The committee provided the needed continuity for each worker by being familiar with the predecessor's work. The net result was elimination of repetition, which had become an objectionable but common occurrence.

It was sometimes difficult to keep the Constitution up to date with the rapid progress taking place. In 1909, at the 26th annual meeting, President W. D. Bigelow pointed out that the Association had been continually adopting provisions for the conduct of business. While some of these had been formalized in the Constitution, others were merely reported in the proceedings and had never been compiled. For example, the Constitution at that time did not cover methods for examination of foods and food standards or medicinal plants. The definition of membership in the Constitution referred to fertilizer chemists and officials, whereas the greater proportion of members already were those concerned with food analysis and regulations. The original single committee on fertilizers had already been replaced by 51 referees and associate referees. A Committee on Compilation of Bylaws, with Bigelow as chairman, was appointed to organize the Constitution and establish Bylaws.

The Journal Emerges

Perhaps the most tangible change at this time was the cessation of publication of the proceedings of the AOAC meetings in the bulletins of the Bureau of Chemistry shortly after Wiley's departure from government service. The Department of Agriculture did not withdraw its support from the Association. Carl Alsberg, the new chief of the Bureau of Chemistry, became Secretary of AOAC and retained that position for eight years until his resignation from USDA. Almost 100 Bureau of Chemistry personnel attended the 1912 meeting -- over 50% of the delegates; state representation comprised about 25%. However, since legal restrictions precluded further printing of the proceedings in the Bureau bulletins, the Association was faced with the serious problem of finding a means of publishing the material. This was especially important since the approved methods which had been published as Bureau of Chemistry bulletins were now generally regarded as official under both state and federal regulatory laws, and chemists needed all possible information available to carry out their duties.

The proceedings of the thirtieth convention were not published in 1914 because of lack of funds. However, President E. F. Ladd, Secretary Alsberg, and many others felt that it was imperative that a means be found to publish the work of the Association promptly if it were to continue to make progress. Meanwhile, the organization struggled with the idea of initiating some sort of general publication. A committee was appointed to investigate the possibilities. The report of this committee and the results of questionnaires sent to chemists to determine if a new journal would be a viable undertaking were not encouraging. Of the 50 letters sent to chemists for opinions, 25 replies were returned and only five of these were strongly in favor of a journal. Only 12 more believed the Association should publish an annual report of proceedings at all. One suggestion was that ACS be asked to publish the proceedings and methods, possibly in one of its journals. The expressed reasons for so little support were the expense involved and the fact that a number of chemical journals were already in existence. Some members were strongly in favor of urging the Department of Agriculture to resume publishing the proceedings. They felt that the work was largely official in character because it was the basis of analytical work for state and federal law enforcement. Despite this, a strong feeling gradually developed at this thirty-first meeting in 1914 that, although there were many financial difficulties in establishing and maintaining a new journal, the fruits of the labors of the agricultural chemists would do justice to its existence.

In his formal report of the meeting on the proposed "Journal of Agricultural Chemistry," Alsberg presented a detailed proposal which had been submitted by Waverly Press of Baltimore, a respected subsidiary of Williams & Wilkins Company, publishers of several other prestigious scientific research journals. The firm agreed to publish a quarterly journal to be restricted to agricultural, food, and drug chemistry, and to contain at least 600 pages per volume. They would edit manuscripts, print, bind, publish, solicit subscriptions and advertising, and distribute the journals, paying all expenses. Authors were to receive no pay, and all material was to be submitted to the managing editor before publication. This last provision guaranteed that questionable advertising would not be permitted, which was a concern expressed by some.

The contribution from the Association was to allow use of its name in a legitimate manner to solicit subscriptions and advertisements, to furnish a list of possible subscribers, and to help further the interests of the journal by other reasonable means. The subscription price was to be set at $5 with a special rate of $4 for members.

A formula was stated for payment of part of any profit to AOAC after the publishers recouped their expenses and a 10% profit. The Association was committed to pay any deficit up to $1000 during any given 12 month period for a period of five years.

There was a great deal of discussion on the report; every possible alternative was presented, including the resumption of publication by USDA. The problem of financing was of paramount importance. Dues, at this time, were $2 per individual member. It was suggested that individual dues be abolished in favor of either the purchase of subscriptions, or payment of dues by the official state and federal groups represented in the membership, in order to raise $25, the amount needed from each organization. Since it was obviously impossible to agree on the details of so important an undertaking as the inauguration of a new journal by debate in a general meeting, a motion was advanced and passed unanimously, authorizing the Executive Committee to publish the proceedings of the Association, either as a single volume or as a quarterly, including the methods. A second motion was then passed to amend the Bylaws to give the Executive Committee authority to resolve the question of annual dues and the amount to be assessed.

By the beginning of the next annual convention in November 1915, President C. H. Jones was able to state in his presidential address that "the Association now has a quarterly publication and our deliberations, printed in a most attractive form, will soon be placed promptly at our disposal." This auspicious announcement was made possible in such a short time as a result of the expeditious and efficient manner in which the Executive Committee, under Alsberg's leadership as Secretary/Treasurer, had carried out their assignment. They had canvassed all the potential publishers for the project and decided that the Williams & Wilkins Company would still be the best choice. Alsberg had stated in his original report the previous year that this company had a great deal of experience in publishing scientific journals. The terms and conditions were quite similar to those which had been stated earlier. Essentially, AOAC agreed to supply manuscripts ready to print, as well as methods. They were also obligated for 200 subscriptions. The Williams & Wilkins Company would be responsible for producing and mailing the journal and handling the financial accounts. With an estimated cost of $3000 for a 600 page volume, the publisher assumed responsibility for $2000 and AOAC for $1000. A profit-sharing arrangement was made for that time when a surplus might be seen. The contract for five years, subject to renewal, was signed by the president of AOAC.

Three numbers of the first volume were already issued by the 1915 meeting at which the report was given. Since no proceedings had been published since the meeting of 1912, there was a large backlog of material. These first three numbers covered the reports of the 1913 and most of the 1914 meetings.

The subscriptions and consequently the finances also got off to a commendable beginning. The Journal had 480 subscribers plus over 100 obtained by the publisher, which made a total of about 600 before the end of the first year, with the number steadily increasing. There were also about eight or nine pages of advertising which had been carefully screened by the Executive Committee. The Executive Committee was very hesitant about accepting advertising at all and relented only on the condition that AOAC had absolute control over what would be accepted. There was no question that a great deal of advertising could be obtained very easily. The policy adopted excluded advertising from any company which produced a product subject to any laws that any member of the Association had the responsibility of enforcing. This limited the advertising essentially to manufacturers of supplies, analytical instruments, glassware, and books, and eliminated such things as feeds, foods, drugs, etc.

The subscription list already included Canada, South America, Australia, and England. Because of the war conditions at the time, there were no subscribers in continental Europe, but those countries began to subscribe after peace was declared.

All the work in managing the *Journal of the Association of Official Agricultural Chemists*, as it had been named, was done in the inaugural year by Alsberg's office, under instruction of the Executive Committee. The Bureau of Chem-

istry was consequently continuing to be an important source of support for
AOAC. Alsberg had no objection to handling the details of the earliest issues
because that work had been of a relatively routine nature. After the first year,
however, he rightfully felt that the Association had to make a number of
decisions regarding this important new venture. Up to that point the editorial
job had been to organize the backlog of proceedings and proofread.

There was now a question of editorial policy, because it was generally
understood that the Journal was to be more than a vehicle for publication of
the proceedings and the methods. There had always been a number of
contributed papers at AOAC meetings, and additional manuscripts would
be submitted which had not yet been publicly presented. These would require
critical editorial assessment and often delicate decisions on revisions and
suitability for publication. The ire of an author rebuffed was as distasteful
then as now, and Alsberg felt that it should be shared. In response, the
Association membership voted to authorize a Board of Editors of the Journal,
consisting of the Secretary as chairman, and four members to serve for one,
two, three, and four years, respectively, each following appointment to be
for four years. The other four members of the first board were R. E. Doolittle,
J. P. Street, E. F. Ladd, and L. L. van Slyke.

Unfortunately, only a short time elapsed before certain difficulties arose
between the Executive Committee, the Board of Editors, and the publisher.
At the 1917 meeting, Alsberg reported on the trouble. One point of contention was the publisher's report that the first year of publication had ended
with a deficit of $275, which Alsberg disputed but felt could be resolved.
Another was the question of the authority of the Board of Editors in relation
to the authority of the printer/publisher. The specific dispute was over the
publication of the methods of AOAC as a supplement to the Journal. The
publisher disagreed over the exact specifications the Board of Editors wanted.
Alsberg reported that the publisher conceded the point, but then having
conceded, insisted on having the matter arbitrated. The publisher had not
printed the remaining three numbers of Volume 3. The manuscripts had
been withheld because of the dispute which Alsberg felt would also be settled
shortly. Publication had been suspended in May 1917 and, as it turned out,
was not resumed until 1920. Alsberg seemed confident at that time that the
methods would be published in book form about the end of 1917. His
optimism unfortunately was not merited, and the unincorporated AOAC
including about 24 members living in Washington became the defendants
in a lawsuit brought by the printing company in the District of Columbia
Supreme Court in July of 1918. The suit, which threatened the very existence
of the organization, was for $50,000 and was based on breach of contract.
The publisher claimed that the Journal was a very successful venture and the

printer would sustain the great loss of anticipated profit during the remainder of the five year contract and the optional renewal period. The projected loss, it maintained, was due to AOAC withholding manuscripts. Fortunately, the suit was dismissed after several years, but not without causing much frustration for those in the Association who were responsible for the Journal. There was also a fee of $500 which had to be paid to the lawyers representing the Association.

It was evident to Alsberg at the end of the first year that the Journal had excellent prospects for being self-supporting. The first publisher, based on statements in the law suit, felt that the publication was a profitable venture. Hence, it was perfectly reasonable that AOAC should continue publication by alternative means. Arrangements were made with a new printer under substantially altered conditions. This printer was to handle only the printing and to be paid a specific price set by short term contracts because of the constantly varying costs. Responsibility for all other details including control of money and other business matters remained in Alsberg's office. As a result of this new arrangement, it was finally possible to continue the issues for Volume 3, beginning with the conclusion of the 1915 proceedings, in 1920. The publisher refused to relinquish the list of subscribers and advertisers, making it necessary to establish a whole new list of subscribers and to search for those subscribers who were still due back issues of Volume 3. Advertisements were placed in other scientific journals to help locate subscribers, as well as companies who were owed advertising space. New advertising copy had to be obtained. The Board of Editors and their staff made a major effort to fulfill all the obligations remaining because of the lapse in producing the Journal as scheduled. During the next few years, in spite of a respectable subscription list of around 800, the Journal operated at a deficit, with confused financial reports because of AOAC's obligation to supply back issues and free advertising. The Journal was now receiving orders from all over the world, including many countries on the European continent. However, individual subscriptions were lagging, and the officers of AOAC, at every opportunity, made a point of urging the members to subscribe to and publicize the Journal.

Fortunately, the first edition of the *Official and Tentative Methods of Analysis* (1920), referred to as the Book of Methods, was published in the same manner as the Journal; that is, all editorial and business matters except the actual printing were handled by Alsberg's office in the Bureau of Chemistry. The volume was an immediate success, and it appeared that the surplus profits from its sale would easily cover the deficit incurred by the Journal. Three thousand copies were printed and sold, and 1000 additional copies were printed the next year. About 10% of the Journal orders were from countries other than the United States and Canada, a gratifying indication of the acceptance of the Association and its work in countries beyond the membership area. The Book of Methods also had a good reception in other countries.

In June 1921, the duties of Secretary/Treasurer of the Association, as well as chairman of the Board of Editors, were taken over by R.W. Balcom. After presenting his first report as chairman, Balcom moved that the practice of having the secretary of the Association serve also as chairman of the Board of Editors be discontinued. With the chairman serving essentially as managing editor, his duties would increase greatly as soon as previous proceedings were published and new contributed papers would have to be reviewed and accepted or rejected. Also, it would be a much more flexible arrangement if the editor could be replaced without changing the secretary. The motion adopted provided that the chairman of the Board of Editors be elected for a period of four years (the same as other members). Balcom remained as chairman of the Board of Editors; and W.W. Skinner of the Bureau of Chemistry became the new Secretary/Treasurer. The Bureau provided not only a good portion of the Board, but also support, in the persons of Nellie A. Parkinson and later Marian E. Lapp who, as associate editors, did much of the actual editorial work. The Journal was now firmly established, leaving the main problem of getting individual support from members. Each college, experiment station, bureau, or board still paid dues of $5 a year to defray the cost of the meetings and other incidentals of operating the Secretary's office. A subscription to the Journal was not included in the dues, as many seemed to think.

In 1923 the first contributed papers began to appear in the Journal. The proceedings had taken the initial 5 volumes, but things were finally brought up to date with the elimination of the long delay between meetings and the publication of the activities. This, of course, made the Journal a more attractive investment to those who were anxious to know as soon as possible what actions had occurred at the meeting. A policy of printing the committee reports in the first issue was adopted, and high quality contributed papers were solicited.

The following year, Balcom suggested that the volume numbers of the Journal be adjusted to coincide with the calendar year. Until that time, each volume had carried the partial proceedings of two annual conventions. Volume 8 was expanded to six issues, and Volume 9, under the new system adopted the following year, contained the full proceedings of one meeting. The Journal at this time was maintaining a subscription list of about 800 with minor fluctuations. The editors and presidents of the Association in their annual reports and addresses were perennially urging and cajoling the membership to increase their support by purchasing individual subscriptions and convincing others to do so. Various factors including economic depression held the subscription list down until 1942 when it finally passed the 1000 mark. From then on, steady increases occurred; the present subscription list is about 4300, with 50% from outside the United States.

Numerous improvements occurred in the format and content of the Journal over the years. Some ideas have been tried and then dropped. In 1928, two new sections, "Book Reviews" and "New Books," were introduced. The decision in 1924 to eliminate advertising from the Journal was later rescinded, and an ambitious campaign to solicit advertising was instituted because of economic contingencies. The practice of supplying free reprints to authors to encourage submission of papers was instituted in 1924 but was later discontinued because of the expense. Until 1928 only certain papers presented at the meetings were accepted for publication on the basis of editorial merit. Beginning in 1928, all research papers presented at the meeting were accepted as contributed papers, and the new policy also provided for the acceptance of contributed papers not presented at the meeting. Preference was given to research in analytical chemistry, but all research in the field of agricultural chemistry was considered. This policy of blanket acceptance of any paper given at the meeting has since been reversed; all contributions, including Associate Referee reports, are now subject to critical peer review with no guarantee of automatic acceptance.

The Journal management has been somewhat ambivalent about the question of having an editorial policy and editorials. In Volume 13, the Board of Editors inaugurated a new editorial policy in which it "proposed to present an editorial or series of editorials on current scientific work and on the activities of the Association of Official Agricultural Chemists." The writers were to be chosen from the Association membership and represent only their opinion. These unsigned editorials appeared for only two years and were discontinued. In the 1932 report of the Editorial Board, Chairman Skinner stated that the policy of no editorials and no abstracts would be continued.

In 1936, Journal publication dates were again adjusted, with the first number of the year moved to January 1 so that the methods changes could be available as soon as possible after the October meeting. Meanwhile, Journal size was growing and the editors were gradually devoting more space to contributed articles and book reviews.

Wartime conditions in the early 1940s created temporary financial and distribution problems. In 1941, a notice was received from postal officials stating no further deliveries to belligerent or occupied countries and that all foreign shipments might have to be discontinued. Many copies of the Journal and of the Book of Methods were subsequently lost in the mail, which created further economic hardship in addition to the curtailment of foreign subscriptions. The annual meetings were cancelled in 1942 and again in 1945. This had not occurred since the cancellation of the 1918 meeting, due to the first World War. The business of the Association for those two meetings was conducted by mail. Because of these cancellations and also because many Associate Referees were engaged in the war effort, the Journal size was markedly diminished for those years. However, all reports submitted were published.

In spite of the fact that the Journal has not been self-sustaining during most of its history, the high quality has been continuosly maintained and upgraded.

By 1953, the annual volume was over 1200 pages and AOAC employed a full-time assistant editor. An editorial complaint during that period was that some referees were submitting both a report and a contributed paper on the same subject. The "publish or perish" syndrome was apparently causing this additional problem. However, the amount of reliable and worthwhile information being submitted for publication was steadily increasing, and Journal space was at a premium. To alleviate some of this pressure, a two-column format was introduced in 1958. This provided a more modern overall appearance and allowed for the use of slightly smaller type, with a consequent saving of space.

In 1963, a section entitled "For Your Information" was added to each issue. This interesting and informative feature presented current information on the affairs of the Association, related meetings, personnel activities, and other items which might appear in a newsletter or similar publication. This section still serves a very useful function in bringing such information to the attention of Journal readers.

Several changes and additions were made in the early 1960s. A set of "Instructions to Authors" on preparation of acceptable manuscripts was published in the August 1962 issue and has been reprinted periodically. The number of issues was increased from four to six per year, since the size had almost doubled from the 600 pages per year of the earlier volumes. An abstract was an added requisite to accompany each paper so that it could be used for direct publication by abstracting services. All methods were required to be written in the general style of *Official Methods of Analysis* to simplify the elaborate re-editing necessary for publication in the book.

The sequence of publishing the transactions of the annual meeting was again revised so that the first issue would include Referee and Associate Referee assignments, reports of the committees, and General Referee reports, as well as "Changes in Methods" and special addresses given at the general session. There have been further revisions in the sequence of publishing the transactions, which has never been static for very long. At that time, the provision was introduced requiring the scientific review of Associate Referee reports as well as contributed papers. In commenting on the actions of the Editorial Board of the Journal at that time, Dr. Daniel Banes, the chairman, stated: "During the past several years the Journal has been undergoing a gradual change from a record of the actions of AOAC, supplemented by papers on related subjects, to a truly scientific publication. The actions of the Editorial Board are intended to aid and hasten this transition so that the Journal may accomplish its part in the general improvement of the Association."

The first cumulative index covered the proceedings from 1884 to 1929 and was issued as Number 4 of Volume 17 in 1934. Since then, it has been kept up to date with the periodic supplement appearing every 10 or 15 years, depending usually on the financial exigencies at the time. The title of the Journal was changed in 1965 to *Journal of the Association of Official Analytical Chemists* to reflect the change in name of the Association.

AOAC has been most fortunate in its choice of editors of the Journal. Although the organizational structure and titles of the editors and staff of the Journal have gone through many changes, the quality has been consistently maintained and improved. Management and policy have been chiefly the responsibility of the editor, chairman of an editorial board, or an editorial board as a group at various times. The responsibility assumed and the amount of time and effort spent in these voluntary positions varied with interest and ability of the incumbents. Some were most interested in seeing that finances were properly managed and that all official actions were properly recorded, while others were skilled writers and were interested in improving the quality of papers. All, of course, had the primary responsibility of accepting or rejecting manuscripts.

However, from the beginning, the actual work of producing the Journal, including preparing the copy, checking and verifying, proofreading, and many other production tasks, has been performed by a succession of very capable people serving as assistant, associate, or managing editors. The first was the previously mentioned Nellie A. Parkinson who served as an associate editor until 1920 when she left to take a position with ACS to become one of the editors of *Chemical and Engineering News*. She was succeeded by Marion

Lapp (later Mrs. Otis) who served until her retirement in 1944. Miss Lapp also helped edit the early editions of *Official and Tentative Methods of Analysis*, and was called out of retirement in 1950 to assist with the preparation of the seventh edition. Katherine Ronsaville became Assistant Editor in 1945, when the position was first put on the AOAC payroll. All her predecessors had been federal employees. When she left in 1951, Ruth Groesbeck filled the position for just one year.

In 1953, Helen Reynolds became the first assistant editor with a degree in chemistry and laboratory experience, part of which had been gained in the U.S. Food and Drug Administration laboratories. Miss Reynolds served in various editorial staff capacities including that of editor, the title she held until resigning from the Journal staff in 1982. Initially employed by AOAC in 1953, Miss Reynolds returned to FDA in 1960 for better career advancement opportunities. Fortunately for AOAC, one of her FDA responsibilites established in 1961 was to act as managing editor of the Journal and various other AOAC publications. She was given the title of editor in 1967 and gradually specialized her activities to managing the review of manuscripts, implementing and developing policy, and editing selected materials. Subsequent members of the editorial staff were all required to have degrees in chemistry or biology and some laboratory experience. When AOAC became independent in 1977, the Association again became responsible for hiring its own editorial staff.

When Helen Reynolds resigned as Journal editor, the ad hoc search committee to find a new editor concluded that the most efficient procedure was to choose a panel of five co-editors, each to handle a designated group of subjects in which he or she was actively involved. Subject categories were divided into agricultural materials; food contaminants and biological methods; residues and elements; food composition and additives; and drugs, colors, cosmetics, and forensic sciences; this new arrangement has proved satisfactory.

In the early years of the Journal and the Book of Methods, business matters (subscription fulfillment, book sales, arrangements for the annual meeting, etc.) were handled by the assistant editor or the staff of the AOAC secretary. Eventually, however, the work increased so that a full-time staff member was needed. In 1946, Rosalind Hicks (later Mrs. Pierce) became the first full-time business manager of AOAC, a position she held with distinction for 33 years until her retirement in 1980. "Rosie," as she was affectionately known throughout the Association, was legendary for her loyalty and devotion to AOAC and even more for her delightful charm and warmth of personality. For some years she not only conducted all the business affairs of the Association but also arranged the details of the annual meeting and registered all the attendees, most of whom she could greet by name. By mid-1950s, a continued increase in the business affairs of AOAC necessitated a full-time assistant in the business office, and the staff grew steadily to its present level. Again, at the time that AOAC became independent of FDA management, which was also the time of Rosie's retirement, the trend toward contracts and other complex funding arrangements warranted the development of a position as comptroller.

The Analysts' Bible

Keeping pace with the development of the Journal and often providing much needed financial buttressing was the book, *Official Methods of Analysis of the AOAC*. The second edition of the book of methods was published in 1925 and was again very well received. The initial printing of 3000 was exhausted in October 1927. Two thousand additional copies were printed since the intention was to revise the book only every 5 years, and include all changes approved at the convention and published annually in the Journal.

When the third edition appeared in 1930, it contained some radical innovations, the most visible of which was the use of abbreviations and symbols for the elements and formulas for most of the chemical compounds. The tables were edited and shortened. The obvious problem prompting this ingenuity was that the amount of information was expanding rapidly and any enlargement in the size of the volume increased the cost of publication. An equivalent of 207 pages of new material was added with an actual expansion of only 58 pages, including a new section on bioassay of drugs. At this time, it was also decided to insert headings for a number of materials on which no information appeared in the book, with the implication that the Association still had a long way to go and did not intend to stand still. These headings included bacteriological tests, marine products, nuts and nut products, radioactivity, fibers, paper and paper-making, and vitamins. The normal revisions, of course, were also included. This edition was so well received, Secretary/Treasurer Skinner reported at the 1933 meeting that, in spite of the economic depression at the time, AOAC would be able to pay in cash for the first printing of 5000 copies of the fourth edition of the book.

The fourth edition was published on schedule in 1935 and contained the official and tentative additions, deletions, and corrections for the five year period with no striking changes in format or coverage. The price to members was set at $4 rather than the anticipated $5 because the Association was in good financial condition in spite of the economic depression and did not need to make a profit. The list of chapters entered by name only with no methods was gradually shrinking because of the cooperation of members concerned with their study. The excellent reception and increased demand for the fourth edition persuaded the Editorial Board to print 7000 copies of the fifth edition. Because of continuing growth in methods output due to the expansion of the work, the editors were hard-pressed to keep the book at a size which could still be sold at a reasonable price. Some saving of space was effected in the fifth edition by partly eliminating the articles "a", "an" and "the."

Regardless of the heroic attempts to conserve space, the size of the book had nearly doubled in the 20 years of its existence. A major additional demand for new and improved methods for foods, drugs, and cosmetics had been triggered by the recent revision of the legislation covering those products. Sales of this edition were excellent, although prevailing wartime conditions resulted in the loss of many overseas sales and also physical losses of volumes in the mail, much the same as the Journal had experienced during this period. The 7000 copies were completely sold by February 1944 and orders for over 800 more could not be filled until the new revision appeared. Apparently, much of the increased demand was due to the references made to the Association's methods in connection with government activities, especially federal contract specifications issued during the war. The implementation of the Federal Food, Drug and Cosmetic Act and amendments, of course, also established a need for AOAC methods in the enforcement of FDA's new responsibilities.

Henry A. Lepper replaced Skinner as chairman of the Editorial Board for the 1945 sixth edition. In this edition, the chapter on paints, varnishes, and constituent materials was deleted; the American Society for Testing and Materials had this area very well covered, and applicable AOAC methods were incomplete and out of date with little or no work in progress. This edition incorporated a new chapter on extraneous materials to enforce the section of the new Food, Drug and Cosmetic Act prohibiting the presence of insect and rodent filth in foods. The scientists of FDA developed a whole new area of quantitative biology based on the isolation of filth elements, using the Wildman trap flask. Nine thousand copies of the edition were printed and 5000 were sold the first year; the second year all but 650 of the remaining 4000 were sold. A new service was initiated, offering annual reprints of changes in methods to purchasers of the book who requested them. Over 6000 of the buyers took advantage of the offer. Several offset reprints of 1000 each were needed to satisfy the demand for the sixth edition and about 13 000 copies were sold. There had never been a question of the validity or value of AOAC methods, but this latest reception of *Official Methods of Analysis* again demonstrated their worldwide acceptance.

One notable difference in the seventh edition was the change in the complete title of the volume from "Official and Tentative Methods of Analysis of the AOAC" to "Official Methods of Analysis of the AOAC." Until this time all methods had been classified as either "tentative," "official first action," or "official final action," each change in designation requiring at least one year's time lapse. In 1948, on the recommendation of the Committee on Classification of Methods, the Bylaws were amended to eliminate the "tentative" classification and designate methods as "first action," or "official."

This action was taken because a court case based on a "tentative method" had been lost. However, the one year lapse before the designation can be changed was retained. This simplified the procedure while still retaining the guarantee of reliability of methods. Three chapters, naval stores, leather, and tanning materials, were deleted, but there were notable increases in the chapters on coloring matters and enzymes in addition to the normal growth due to new method adoption. Further refinements in the system of abbreviations continued to provide some of the needed space for the rapidly growing volumes, but the eighth edition in 1955 was the last in which the page size could be held to its original 6 by 9 inches. Also, some space was saved in this edition through the deletion of many unnecessary methods and variations. This was possible, in large part, because of the introduction of instrumental techniques such as spectrophotometry and chromatography. This edition was the first to be placed on the U.S. Government list for procurement under contract.

The book of official methods had now reached a point where size made the publication of the next edition in the same format impractical. The Journal had switched to the two-column page and this had been very well accepted. Dr. William Horwitz, in his capacity as general chairman of the Editorial Board, recommended this format for the ninth edition of the book.

With the slightly larger page size and use of two columns it was possible to reduce the number of pages in the ninth edition substantially, allowing for future growth. The chapter on soils was eliminated because the Association felt the subject was more appropriately covered by a specialized society. Numerous instrumental methods were added, continuing a trend that was to increase rapidly with each future revision. The chapter on metals, other elements, and residues in foods was increased in size as a result of the increasing demand for reliable methods for determining organic pesticide residues in foods. This demand arose from the passage of the Miller Amendment to the Food, Drug and Cosmetic Act in 1954, which required that tolerances be set and methods of analysis for residues be available for residues of pesticides in food. The Miller Amendment presented a further challenge to AOAC, since only eight such methods had been adopted in the five years between editions. The Food Additives Amendment of 1958 had a similar effect in increasing the workload of the Association and hence, the productivity, as reflected in the growth in size of the methods book. Also, the ninth edition had to be reprinted to satisfy the demand after the initial printing of 12 000 was exhausted. There were no drastic changes in the tenth edition because the type from the previous edition was stored and reused. This allowed a substantial saving in the cost of typesetting and proofreading, but resulted in a slightly poorer quality because of a slight difference in impression

J.D. Wildman and his trap flask, about 1939.

between the new and old type. Since this also restricted substantial rearrangement of sectional materials, it was not recommended that the type be stored again for the next edition.

For the eleventh edition, General Referees remained responsible for their chapters, but special reviewers were also selected to review some subject areas which needed special attention and to convey suggestions to the appropriate referees. A new section on "Laboratory Safety" was added and potentially hazardous operations and materials used in the methods were cross-referenced to it by a cautionary statement. ACS Chemical Abstracts Registry numbers were added in the index to allow direct access to the Chemical Abstracts information system. A new chapter titled "Natural Poisons" was added and three new chapters on additives were formed from material taken from other chapters. Other sections were rearranged or modified, and the new methods of the previous five years were again added. A style manual used for the eleventh edition was later revised and made available for general use.

Innovations in the twelfth edition in 1975, aside from the inclusion of about 250 new methods which had been adopted since the previous publication, included indexing by section number rather than page number, a section on forensic science, and various reorganizations. This edition was prepared by a computer-driven photocomposition process using punched paper tape which could be saved and used in the preparation of the next edition. The "Changes in Methods" in the Journal were also to be printed the same way so they could be integrated easily into the methods book. Seventeen thousand copies were printed. In October 1978, the Board of Directors approved the donation of up to 500 copies of the twelfth edition of *Official Methods of Analysis* to the United Nations for their distribution to bench chemists in developing countries. While distribution problems prevented this plan from being carried out completely, hundreds of copies of the book of methods have been donated to these countries.

The thirteenth edition of *Official Methods of Analysis* was kept to a single volume only by again increasing the page size. Users of the book, in a survey made by AOAC, expressed an overwhelming preference to have the compendium continued as one volume. A designation of "surplus methods" had been adopted in the eleventh edition, whereby space was saved in future issues by not reprinting certain methods which were thought not to be in current use for various reasons, but indicating them only by reference. However, the size of the book continued to grow in spite of this step, the deletion of some methods, and a decline in the number of new methods approved compared with the twelfth edition. Again, instrumental methods were prominent in the new additions. Liquid chromatography, which had not appeared previously, accounted for six percent of the new methods in the thirteenth edition. In the preface, Dr. William Horwitz, the editor of this edition as well as the five preceding it, presented data which vividly illustrated the major role of instrumental methods in the 1975 and 1980 editions. The use of a wide variety of instruments of diverse design from many competing manufacturers has created a whole new problem area for AOAC and the best ways to standardize instrumental procedures in the methods book has become a significant area of study.

The fourteenth edition of *Official Methods of Analysis* will be published as part of the centennial celebration of AOAC.

Other Publications

The quirks of fate which began when USDA refused to continue to publish AOAC proceedings and culminated in the Williams & Wilkins lawsuit, and which forced AOAC into the publishing business, led to a gradually more active role in this area. The Journal and *Official Methods of Analysis* have been continuously published for almost 70 years, but there have been numerous other ventures with varying degrees of economic success. The earliest was the joint publication in 1923, with the American Public Health Association (APHA) of *Standard Methods of Milk Analysis of the American Public Health Association and the Association of Official Agricultural Chemists.* The bacteriological methods were supplied by APHA, and AOAC provided the official chemical procedures. This was the first of many editions, but the arrangement was discontinued in the early sixties. A much more ambitious undertaking was the third revision and publication of H. W. Wiley's three-volume work, *Principles and Practices of Agricultural Analysis.* Several years before his death, Wiley had begun the revision and had completed Volume 1 in 1935. When his health declined later that year to the point where he felt he could no longer continue the project, he offered to AOAC the copyrights to the revisions of Volumes 2 and 3 under certain conditions if they would complete the task and publish the revised books. After some negotiating, AOAC accepted the proposal and assigned volunteer experts from among its members to edit and revise Volumes 2 and 3. *Principles and Practices* was meant by Wiley to provide the analyst with significant statistical and historical material on analytical methods and to act as a handbook for the interpretation of the analyst's findings. In this way, it could be considered a valuable adjunct to the book of methods, and AOAC members felt that they could accept the offer. The books had been very well received with excellent reviews on first publication. However, the revision met with a very poor reception, in part perhaps because of the very bad economic conditions. The Editorial Board felt that the main problem was that the publisher was extremely apathetic in advertising the book and promoting sales. At any rate, Volume 2 sold few copies and the Association was forced to give up the project after the revision of Volume 3 was almost completed. The Editorial Committee for *Principles and Practices* was dissolved in 1935.

Little further activity occurred in this area until the past 15 or 20 years. In 1956, AOAC published a commemorative brochure in connection with the celebration of the fiftieth anniversary of the first Food and Drug Law and the Meat Inspection Act. It contained reprints of the tributes to Wiley which were made at the time of his death, an address on the work of AOAC by Henry Lepper, a list of past presidents, and other facts about the Association.

Distribution and interest was limited.

In 1962, the Association began the publication of monographs in cooperation with the Food and Drug Administration. The first of these was *A Manual of Cosmetic Analysis*, by Sylvan H. Newburger. It contained analytical methods for all the major forms of cosmetics and their constituents. General techniques for chromatography and ultraviolet and infrared spectrophotometry were covered and pertinent infrared spectra were presented. A new edition, significantly updated and expanded, was published in 1977.

The second was *Micro-Analytical Entomology for Food Sanitation Control*, by O. L. Kurtz and Kenton L. Harris. This major work contained over 600 pages and more than 800 illustrations, including more than 300 reproductions of authentic photomicrographs of insect structures and fragments. The photographs were used in detecting insect infestation in food and identifying the specific insect, thus pinpointing the source and legal responsibility for the contamination. Because of involvement of FDA and their personnel, these publications and many of those to follow could not, under provisions of federal laws, be copyrighted. Both of these were very successful ventures and proved extremely useful to the scientific communities they served.

In 1962, Paul Clifford, former editor of the Journal, began to prepare a handbook of the organization and operation of AOAC. This was published in 1963 and has gone through four revisions since then. It contains a wealth of information about AOAC, including a short history, objectives, membership provisions, organizational structure, procedures for developing and adopting methods, and general activities. Another 1963 release was the reprint as a separate booklet of *Infrared, Ultraviolet and Visible Absorption Spectra of Some USP and NF Reference Standards and Their Derivatives*, by Hayden et al. which had appeared in the November 1962 issue of the Journal.

The growing recognition of the importance of proper statistical design of collaborative experiments and statistical analysis in interpretation of data led to the presentation of several special evening lectures in 1961 and 1962 by Dr. W. J. Youden, of the National Bureau of Standards, on statistics and their specific application to AOAC collaborative studies. These were so enthusiastically received that Youden was asked to write a manual on the subject. The result was *Statistical Techniques for Collaborative Tests*, published in 1967. As Dr. Horwitz stated in the preface, "Dr. Youden, initially a chemist but later a statistician, had the knack of setting down, in understandable terms, statistical principles that can be applied directly with simple mathematics and analytical geometry to the basic AOAC problem of variability of methods of analysis." The lectures and the publication had a profound influence on improving both the quality and the interpretation of subsequent collaborative studies. The booklet was revised and reprinted in 1970, and in 1975 it was combined with a work by E.H. Steiner which had been published in England by the British Food Manufacturing Industries Research Association. The British Association assigned the copyright of Steiner's "Planning and Analysis of Results of Collaborative Tests" to AOAC, which published the composite as the *Statistical Manual of the AOAC*. Reprintings were authorized in 1981 and 1982, and this manual continues to be a best seller for AOAC.

In 1966, the Association published *Principles of Regulatory Drug Analysis* by Dr. Daniel Banes. This book explains the chemical principles on which the methods of drug analysis are based, and filled a need which had long existed. Another volume by Banes, *A Chemist's Guide to Regulatory Drug Analysis*, was published in 1974 and was specifically directed at chemists concerned with the analysis of drugs from the standpoint of regulations and quality control. This publication had the distinction of being the first AOAC book published by computer-assisted photocomposition.

With a major portion of AOAC activity involved in the publication of the Journal and the Book of Methods it became increasingly evident that the detailed uniform style for preparing manuscripts should be made available to prospective contributors. Consequently, the first edition of the *AOAC Style Manual* was published in 1972. This was revised in 1975 and a further revision was combined with the *Handbook for AOAC Members*, published in 1982.

Increased financial pressure on the AOAC in the 1970s, resulting from the formal severence of FDA's financial subsidization of the Association, which is recounted elsewhere, gave additional impetus to the publications program. Production, publication, editing, and distribution of scientific manuals was a valuable service which AOAC could supply to acquire financial support for other activities. AOAC has entered into numerous contracts, primarily with government agencies, for assistance with training and reference books.

In 1976, the Association published and distributed the *FDA Bacteriological Analytical Manual* (BAM), fourth edition, for the Food and Drug Administration. It also published and distributed the *EPA Manual of Chemical Methods for Pesticides and Devices* for the Environmental Protection Agency. Both were issued in looseleaf form, and supplements were also handled by AOAC. The Association also, under contract, provided the technical review and distributions of the *EPA Pesticides Formulation Manual*, as well as the revision of

EPA manuals on pesticide residues in human and environmental materials, and on quality control, and the periodic supplements.

Three special publications in 1978 included the fifth edition of BAM, *FDA Training Manual for Analytical Entomology in the Food Industry*, and *Mycotoxins Mass Spectral Data Bank*. Since then, other such publications have appeared, including the *FDA Food Additives Analytical Manual*. The "International Symposium on Drug Residues in Animal Tissues" presented at the 1977 annual meeting and sponsored jointly by FDA and AOAC was issued as a special reprint. Another symposium on quality assurance, which was held at the 94th annual meeting, was published as a separate volume in 1981 and was so well received that a reprinting was authorized the following year.

Several times during the history of the Association, the suggestion had been made that a newsletter be authorized, but the Board of Directors had not accepted the idea. Finally, in 1977 the Association inaugurated a 4-page bimonthly bulletin, appropriately christened *The Referee*, for bringing news to all members. *The Referee* has provided a vehicle for furnishing news and information on AOAC meetings and activities, and related events to the members much more rapidly than could be possible in the Journal. The publication has been enthusiastically received as attested by the statement in the 1979 report of the Editorial Board: "The Board affirmed unanimously that *The Referee* is an effective and valuable asset of the Association. The Board approved expansion of the *The Referee* from 6 to 10 issues per year." The number of pages of the newsletter has also been increased for most issues.

The Association's ambitious publishing activities continue to complement its methods research and validation activities.

The Quiet Times

The regulatory responsibilities that resulted from the 1906 Food and Drug Law were carried out by the Bureau of Chemistry of USDA until 1927. At that time, it was decided that research and regulatory activities needed to be separated. Consequently the Food, Drug, and Insecticide Administration was made a separate unit of USDA to conduct the regulatory work. The name was later changed to Food and Drug Administration. FDA remained part of USDA until 1940, when it was transferred to the newly created Federal Security Agency. In 1953 it became part of the Department of Health, Education and Welfare (later Health and Human Services). Because AOAC methods were so important to regulatory work, the chief participation in AOAC gradually passed from USDA to FDA. W.W. Skinner of USDA, who became Secretary/Treasurer of AOAC in 1922, remained in that position until his retirement from government service in 1943. He was succeeded by Henry A. Lepper of the Food and Drug Administration, who served through 1951 and was followed for a short, interim term by Kenneth L. Milstead, FDA. Milstead was in turn succeeded by William Horwitz, also of the Food and Drug Administration, who remained the AOAC chief executive officer until the Association became a fully independent organization in 1979.

The decades of the 1920s and 1930s were a relatively quiet and uneventful period in AOAC history. By this time the Association was well established, with its work recognized and respected worldwide. The Journal, which was still in its infancy in 1920, made much progress during the next decade under the guidance of R. W. Balcom, who served as chairman of the Board of Editors during most of this critical time until 1927. The gradual but steady upgrading was continued by R. B. Deemer and others. The financial condition of the Association was elevated from the state of bankruptcy which existed around 1920, caused by settlement of the printer's suit, to a sound position by 1931 due to the astute management of Secretary/Treasurer W. W. Skinner. The exigencies of the Great Depression era were felt by AOAC as well as by other organizations during the 1930s and early 1940s but the activities continued. Although there was no extensive growth in the amount of work which could be done, the Association accomplished a great deal by expanding its cooperation with other groups that had similar interests. This provided a means of conserving precious time and resources by eliminating the duplication of effort. Liaisons were initiated to varying degrees with the Crop Protection Institute of the National Research Council, the American Society for Testing and Materials, the American Public Health Association, and others. The Association still maintains active liaisons with these and many others.

Increased interest in the new field of vitamin chemistry began in the early 1920s and soon stimulated enthusiastic interest and consequent research activity by AOAC chemists. A contributed paper, "The Vitamins from the Viewpoint of the Official Chemists," was presented at the 1931 meeting by H. C. Sherman of Columbia University. The urgency for vitamin methods research, as well as research on the nature of the vitamins, was becoming increasingly apparent to the Association. Spectrophotometric methods, although prohibitively expensive for most laboratories at the time, were recognized as the probable best solution to vitamin analysis. During this period, new analytical processes such as precipitation with organic complexes and potentiometric titrations were evolving. Although they were recognized as useful and were investigated by AOAC referees, their introduction into AOAC official methods was slow. This situation often evoked criticism, but was in keeping with the traditional AOAC conservatism which has served it so well in the matter of method adoption. While thorough testing was and is a hallmark of all AOAC methods, the Association is committed to investigate and research new techniques as soon as they are available. Symposia on new analytical methods first became a feature of the annual meeting in 1935.

The incorporation of AOAC in 1932 eased fears which had been raised in the minds of the officers by the printer's suit a decade earlier. A similar suit aimed at the officers and individual members could have led to personal economic disaster before incorporation. The Board of Directors of the corporation was designated to include the officers and Executive Committee. Since the depressed economic conditions were of great concern, it was gratifying that the Secretary was able to report, in the wake of the 1932 bank crisis, that practically all AOAC funds had been in secure places and only a very small loss had occurred.

One innovation of the early 1930s was the dividing of the annual meeting into sections to allow for the presentation of more scientific reports. This generated keener interest and more meaningful discussion than had been possible within the general meeting format and has proven highly successful.

Perhaps the most rapidly expanding area of interest in AOAC during this period was drugs. By 1936, there were 22 topics in the drug section, and the number was increasing. Official methods were much in demand, and novel techniques were needed.

The Challenge from the New Food, Drug and Cosmetic Law

A major challenge to the Association, and an event which would profoundly influence and expand its activities, occurred in 1938 with the passage of the revised Federal Food, Drug and Cosmetic Act. The Food and Drug Administration, as well as many consumers, had long advocated and frequently requested an overhaul and expansion of the original Food and Drug Act of 1906. The very first vehement protests had been those of Harvey Wiley in regard to the manner in which the original law was being interpreted to avoid enforcing it as strictly as intended. Loopholes were apparent from the beginning. At the time that the first bill calling for total revision was introduced in the Senate by Senator Copeland in June 1933, the 1906 act had been amended only three times. The Sherley Amendment of 1912 forbade the use of false and fraudulent therapeutic claims on the labels of patent medicines. However, the difficulty in proving fraudulent intent had severely weakened the effectiveness of this provision. In 1913 the Net Weight Act added the requirement that a declaration of quantity appear on the label of all packaged food. Then, in 1930, the McNary-Mapes Amendment, or "Canner's Bill," mandated the promulgation of minimum standards of quality, condition, and fill of containers.

When the Copeland Bill was introduced into the Senate, it had strong support from consumers and many legislators. It was endorsed by President Franklin D. Roosevelt, who early in his new administration had called for a new food and drug law. It also had the same kind of powerful opposition as the earlier law had received from certain segments of the affected industries. Considerable legislative activity ensued during the next five years of debate and several other versions of a revised food and drug law were introduced and eventually discarded. However, it was generally recognized that the 1906 act was very much out of date. During the 30 years it had been in existence, many new products had been introduced, new methods of manufacturing had been adopted, new scientific discoveries had been made, and new sophisticated methods of marketing and advertising, including the radio, had come into widespread use. The billion dollar cosmetic industry had been of relatively little significance in 1906 and was not covered by that law. The existing legislation did not control harmful drugs as long as they were labeled and unadulterated. Devices were not controlled, and legal standards did not exist for many products.

In spite of the obvious desirability and need for reform, the new law might still have fallen by the wayside if it had not been for the efforts of three crusading consumer advocate authors. A. Kallet and F. J. Schlink published *100,000,000 Guinea Pigs* in 1933. This book, which had gone through 33 printings by October 1938, dealt in very specific terms with ineffectiveness of the existing laws to protect the consumer, and cited examples of the serious health problems and instances of fraud which were occurring as a consequence. A second book, *American Chamber of Horrors* by Ruth de Forest Lamb, was subtitled "The Truth About Food and Drugs." It was published in 1936 in the midst of the battle over the adoption of the new law and contained graphic descriptions as well as illustrations of numerous horrible cases of injury and death which had resulted from the use of ineffective or injurious drugs or cosmetics which could not be adequately controlled under the 1906 act and its amendments. These books helped arouse widespread indignation and anger in the public sector and were undoubtedly instrumental in achieving the final victory of the passage of the new Federal Food, Drug and Cosmetic Act of 1938. One other single event which also had a major impact on the public and rallied support for passage of the Copeland Bill was the fatal poisoning of over 100 persons by elixir of sulfanilamide which had been formulated with a poisonous solvent. The need for the testing of drugs for safety before marketing was clearly evidenced by this tragic episode.

A number of important new provisions in the 1938 act served to reinforce and vitally expand the effectiveness of consumer protection. Coverage was extended to cosmetics and to devices, two important groups of commodities which had figured prominently in poisoning and suspected fraud incidents. Provision was included for the establishment of tolerances for "unavoidable" poisonous substances. The frustrating requirement that actual intent to defraud be proven in accusations of drug misbranding was eliminated. Predistribution safety clearance was made a prerequisite for marketing of new drugs. Standards of identity, quality, and fill of container were authorized for foods. The new legislation also authorized factory inspections and added the instrument of court injunction to the previously allowed seizure and prosecution initiatives.

Although this food, drug, and cosmetics law was a vast improvement over the one it served to amend, it did not solve all the problems and was itself subject to amendment in later years. A major updating was begun in 1950 with the appointment by Congress of the Select Committee to Investigate the Safety of Chemicals in Foods under the chairmanship of Congressman James J. Delaney of New York. This committee, which heard testimony and deliberated for two years, was responsible for three major amendments requiring premarket approval of products and put the burden of proof of safety on industry. The first was the Miller Pesticide Chemical Amendment, which was enacted in 1954 and provided for the establishment of tolerances for pesticide chemical residues which might be present as a result of the necessary use of such materials in crop production. The Food Additives Amendment of 1958 recognized the need for the use of some additives and the fact that certain levels of safety could be established. It provided for the designation of maximum allowable amounts in edible products. The "Delaney Clause" was added to prohibit the use of any additive found to induce cancer in humans or experimental animals. The Color Additive Amendment of 1960 was the third important amendment to emanate from the committee hearings. It required that limits be set on amounts of these intentional adulterants in food products. Other amendments have been added to the 1938 act to keep it current as technology changes. Each of these changes, beginning with the initial legislation in 1938, has necessitated the development and testing of new methods and new techniques.

The rapid expansion of government laboratory facilities to help administer the new laws during this period allowed a great number of chemists and other scientists to work within the AOAC framework, along with the state and industry members, in answering the challenge for development of methodology in these new areas. The progress has continued with the investigation and adoption for regulatory analysis of such innovations as automatic analyzers, mass spectroscopy, gas chromatography, liquid chromatography, and column chromatography, and multiresidue analysis systems. Computer control of equipment and computer treatment of data are among the latest technological advances being used to modernize and facilitate the treatment of official samples and reports.

Honors and Awards Program

After Dr. Wiley's death in 1930, he was honored by a special session at the AOAC annual meeting with glowing tributes presented by colleagues, friends, and employees. These were published as his obituary in the first issue of the 1931 volume of the Journal and reprinted in booklet form. The loss of a man who had been a founder, president, secretary, and honorary president of the organization for over 40 years was truly mourned by the members of the Association, and they wished to institute some tangible way to honor his memory and keep it alive. They chose a series of ten annual Wiley Memorial Lectures to be presented by distinguished scientists at the subsequent annual meetings. As the date of the final lecture drew nearer, the Association felt it should decide on a plan for another memorial to the man who had contributed so much. A Committee on Fellowships was appointed in 1937 and suggested several plans, including an undergraduate fellowship, which was adopted with the hope of stimulating interest in the field of agricultural chemistry and encouraging research on problems within the scope of the Association's activities. Three awards were to be presented annually to undergraduates "for the three best presentations, either as theses, compilations, or resumés that may be offered upon any one of the subjects dealt with in the several chapters of the Association's Methods of Analysis." The competition was open to senior class members of accredited colleges or universities in North America. The committee felt that the contest would not only stimulate interest in problems related to agricultural chemistry, but it would also provide a list of new graduates for prospective employers as well as a source of scientific contributions, potentially useful to Associate Referees. A circular announcing the award was distributed, and entries from several colleges were submitted. As a result of the deliberations of the committee in 1939, the first Harvey W. Wiley Memorial Awards were presented in the form of a $300, $200, and $100 award, respectively, to H. F. Snow from Massachusetts Institute of Technology, R. D. Maby of Purdue University, and J. D. Servis of the University of Florida. The awards were presented again to three students in 1940. After these two years, the awards were suspended and not reinstated, possibly because of the disruptions in education and in AOAC affairs occasioned by World War II. Although Wiley was certainly not forgotten, and he was frequently referred to with reverence and respect in presidential addresses, there were no further formal AOAC memorials to him until the fiftieth anniversary of the first Pure Food and Drug Law in 1956. That year, the annual banquet was designated as the Harvey W. Wiley Memorial Banquet and a special brochure or commemorative booklet was issued as the program for the event. In it were reprinted the tributes presented at the time of his death as well as other historical information pertaining to Wiley and AOAC. The Association also helped organize and participated in "The National Meeting to Commemorate the 50th Anniversary of the Basic National Pure Food, Drug, Cosmetic and Meat Inspection Laws in the United States," held in Washington, DC, on June 27, 1956, at which Wiley's contributions were acclaimed. Also, AOAC suggested and was a party to the successful petition for a Wiley commemorative postage stamp issued that year.

During this period of celebration, the Association was again moved to establish a tangible tribute to the memory of Dr. Wiley, one of a viable and continuous nature. The Executive Committee approved the appointment by the president of a Harvey W. Wiley Award Committee to explore the potential for establishing an award and to suggest rules, regulations, and procedures for administration. The report of the committee was approved at the 1956 annual convention, and led to the establishment of "The Harvey W. Wiley Award for Development of Analytical Methods," sponsored by AOAC. Its avowed purpose was to "recognize and encourage the development of outstanding analytical methods for application to problems encompassed by the Official Methods of Analysis of the Association of Official Agricultural Chemists" as well as for methods in general analytical chemistry. The establishment of the award was intended to recognize the essential role of analytical methodology in research as well as product inspection and regulatory control. It was also hoped that the important role of scientists in improving consumer protection and the effective utilization of agricultural commodities would become generally more apparent. An anonymous Wiley Awards Committee was appointed by the president with a membership of six specialists in various fields of the Association's interest to serve on a rotating basis. The president acted as chairman with power to vote in case of a tie. Nominations were solicited from the entire membership and the awards committee was not required to make an award if it felt no suitable candidate was available. The award consisted of $500, an amount since increased to $2500, and a scroll bearing an appropriate description of the accomplishments for which the prize was presented.

The first award went to Lloyd C. Mitchell of the Food and Drug Administration in recognition of 45 years of valuable contributions of methodology and collaborative studies, including the important pioneer work on pesticide multiresidue analysis by paper chromatography. The award has been continued for over 25 years and has annually been presented to an exceptional scientist who has done justice to the memory of its namesake. It is also traditional for the award recipient to deliver a Wiley Award Address at the general session of the annual meeting. These excellent presentations are published in the Journal.

All the early awards were funded from AOAC general funds. However, through the generosity of Harvey Wiley's widow, Anna Kelton Wiley, who presented the Association with a check for $2000 at the banquet in 1962, the Harvey W. Wiley Award Fund was established. The Executive Committee matched the contribution, and designated that the fund would be used for the independent financial support of the Harvey W. Wiley Award for Development of Analytical Methods, established five years earlier, and also for possible future awards, fellowships, scholarships, etc., in Wiley's honor. An immediate campaign was launched to increase the amount in the fund by additional contributions from members and friends. A brochure was composed and distributed by the end of 1963. An additional $8000 was provided by Mrs. Wiley in her will, following her death on January 6, 1964.

When the Executive Committee established the Wiley fund in 1962, it authorized the president to appoint a committee to make recommendations on the type of additional donations accepted and how the fund should be managed. In the meantime it was decided that the general fund would be used for the Wiley Award until the new fund reached a sum that would support it on an annual basis. As the initial new project utilizing the Harvey W. Wiley Award Fund, a scholarship award program was undertaken with a prize of $300 for study at a college or university. The award is made annually to an outstanding junior student who is pursuing a course of study in science, who has a high scholastic average, and who needs financial assistance. The scholarship is awarded for the junior and senior year, so that after the initial award in 1956 to Mr. Stephen L. Taylor, a junior in the Department of Food Science and Technology at Oregon State University, two students each year have been benefiting from the fund. Although the fund showed promise of rapid growth the first few years, donations did not materialize at the expected rate. In 1969, the total worth was still only about $15 000, even though all awards were still being financed by the general treasury of AOAC. The yearly value of the scholarship award was later raised from $300 to $500. The Wiley Award Fund, for some inexplicable reason, never really attracted a substantial amount of money in donations, and in 1973 the Executive Committee voted a continuous annual appropriation of $1500 from the Association's funds to the Wiley Award Fund. This new arrangement provided a mechanism for future awards to be paid from the Wiley Award Fund, which has now accumulated assets sufficient to cover these expenses and is no longer subsidized from general funds.

The Wiley Award Fund Committee was instrumental in establishing an additional award program when it recommended in its 1970 report that "The AOAC Award of Merit" be presented annually for the most outstanding contribution by an Associate Referee. This recommendation, initiated in

1964 by the Committee on Improvement (later the Long Range Planning Committee), was approved by the Executive Committee in 1970, and the first award was made in 1971 to William Plank of the Food and Drug Administration, Brooklyn, NY. The criteria for selecting the winner were established by the Committee on Recommendations of Referees and include ingenuity and originality in method development, design of the collaborative study, statistical analysis considerations, literature review, and abstract content, among others. The actual selection of the winner of what has come to be known as the "Annual Associate Referee Award" is done first by ballot in each of the Methods Committees. The nominees of each individual committee are then considered by all the chairmen acting as members of the Methods Board, who select the award recipient. The certificate is presented at the annual meeting. An additional way to recognize special contributions to the work of AOAC was established in 1972 when the Executive Committee approved the awarding of scrolls, at the annual meeting, to deserving members for outstanding service.

A program of electing Fellows of the AOAC was initiated in the early 1960s. In 1961, the Committee on Improvement proposed that the Association recognize deserving persons by electing them as "Fellows" of AOAC. The Executive Committee adopted this suggestion that year and authorized the establishment of Fellows of AOAC and the appointment of a committee to determine the necessary qualifications and mechanisms of selection. In its report the following year, the Committee on Establishment of Fellows of AOAC proposed that the criteria for election be based on service to the Association in the capacity of Referees, Associate Referees, committee members, and other positions as the primary consideration, as well as scientific accomplishments in areas of interest to the Association. At least ten years of meritorious service were required for nomination for the honor. Any member of the Association could make nominations, which would then be acted on by the Committee on Fellows, consisting of the past president and four anonymous members of the Association appointed by the president for terms of two years, as established by an amendment to the Bylaws in 1963. The initial list of Fellows was rather extensive, since it was decided to include all living past presidents among many other deserving members who qualified for the honor. Subsequent annual groups have generally consisted of between five and ten individuals, awarded certificates in a ceremony at the general session of the annual meeting.

Development of Committee Structures

Although AOAC is more dependent on the continued energetic participation of its total membership than most organizations, it also has always
used a strong ad hoc and standing committee structure to facilitate and
improve the performance of its mission.

Official Methods Board

As previously noted, the Official Methods Committees were established
as early as the first meeting in 1880, before the formal organization of
AOAC, to consider the adoption of methods for fertilizer constituents. These
were soon changed to investigators or referees who conducted the studies and
made recommendations which were evaluated by a Committee on Recommendations. As the scope of subjects covered by the Association's activities
increased, it became apparent that a further reorganization was needed. In
1901, three Committees on Recommendations were appointed to better
evaluate the larger number and different kinds of methods being presented.
These were designated Committees A, B, and C on Recommendations. The
topics under consideration at that time were divided among the three committees in such a manner that related items were grouped as well as possible.
As the Association expanded its interests and adopted new topics, committee
assignments were revised and new topics were added to the groups for which
a Committee on Recommendations was responsible. In 1916 an amendment
to the Constitution established an additional general Committee on Referees
encompassing the other three committees, which were then designated as
subcommittees. The general committee had the duty of reviewing subcommittee reports as well as recommending to the president the names of
prospective Referees and Associate Referees. The following year it was decided
to restructure the referee system with the designation of a General Referee
for certain related groups of subjects and a sufficient staff of Associate Referees
to work with the General Referee in the investigation of important questions
in the field covered. The General Referees were also expected to make
recommendations at the general meeting as well as keep up to date on all
the items relevant to their general subjects. This system of Referee and
Associate Referee responsibilities is still in practice.

In the 1935 report of the Committee on Recommendations of Referees,
Chairman Lepper discussed the continued enlargement of the scope of AOAC
work and the excellent participation of its members, referring particularly
to the reports in the new fields of microbiological and vitamin methods. The

expanded activities were causing problems for the committee and the three subcommittees to resolve in the time available. To alleviate the congestion, Chairman Lepper suggested that the Committee on Recommendations of Referees be enlarged by three members, permitting the formation of a new Subcommittee D, with a reassignment of subjects as deemed advantageous. An amendment to the Constitution was adopted to accommodate this expansion. The committee was enlarged again in 1961 to help relieve the press of work immediately before the annual meeting. The new Subcommittee E consisted primarily of Referees and Associate Referees in the area of traces of chemical contamination or residues, a rapidly expanding area of concern due, in part, to the increasing recognition of the possible hazards from pesticide residues. Subcommittee F was formed by the Executive Committee in 1965. At that time, the membership of the Committee on Recommendations of Referees was expanded to 18 members and a chairman to provide for the new subcommittee, responsible for review of the rapidly increasing number of biological reports and methods. Several other subjects were again reassigned to balance the committee's workload. The latest subcommittee to be added, G, was organized in 1971. The new referee topic of microbial mutagenicity testing, as well as biochemical methods and a number of others, were assigned to this subcommittee. A list of the topics presently under study in the Methods Committees can be found in the annual March issue of the Journal. The Committee on Recommendations of Referees was renamed the Official Methods Board in 1980 to recognize its stature, and the seven subcommittees are now designated as Official Methods Committees. The chairmen of the committees form the Official Methods Board, and the chairman of the Official Methods Board is appointed by the president. These committees still carry on their historical responsibility of providing guidance to the respective referees in their duties, and recommending to the Association the acceptance or rejection of the proposed methods.

Long Range Planning Committee

The Long Range Planning Committee, renamed in 1965, was originally established in 1958 as the Committee on Improvement of AOAC to study the methods development work and make recommendations for its improvement. Since the methods development work is related to every phase of AOAC activity, this committee assumed unique importance in reviewing the performance and responsibilities of the Association and suggesting a wide range of activities to improve the efficiency and the image of AOAC. Many of the procedural and organizational changes discussed elsewhere were originally broached by the Long Range Planning Committee. Among its first recommendations to the Executive Committee were the appointment of liaison committees to work with official, trade, and scientific organizations to obtain better cooperation in the studies of methods; the preparation of a brochure containing detailed statements of the duties and responsibilities of the Associate Referees, General Referees, and subcommittees, and holding a meeting of these members during the annual convention; the consideration of the general application of statistics to collaborative studies; and reorganization of some portions of the Journal. These valuable suggestions were the basis of productive changes and this committee has continued to be a guiding force in upgrading the efficiency of the Association and charting the direction of its expansion into relevant new areas.

The Long Range Planning Committee was the first to advocate the establishment of area chapters. This proposal, contained in the 1966 committee report, was greatly expanded and finally implemented in 1981. Model bylaws for regional sections were developed by the Long Range Planning Committee at the request of the Board of Directors. This venture into affiliated chapters is proving quite successful.

As the AOAC Handbook states, "The Long Range Planning Committee provides guidelines for improved functions and operations of AOAC for growth and stability including organization, funding, membership, methods output, meetings, services, publicity, and communications" and "predicts future trends and events that may affect AOAC." Therefore, it was not surprising that this committee evolved into a major advisory force to the Executive Committee in its reorganizing and restructuring process when the Association was required to become independent of the Food and Drug Administration which had long supported it with funds and personnel.

The activities of the Long Range Planning Committee during that period are treated elsewhere.

Committee on the Constitution

In 1961, the Committee on the Constitution was formed to review and recommend to the Board of Directors revision of the AOAC Bylaws to accommodate changing roles and requirements. It also acts as a check against proposed actions which might conflict with the Bylaws. Until this time, the Bylaws had been altered and expanded numerous times when changes in activities dictated, but there had not been a standing committee to routinely monitor the situation. In its first year the committee made a thorough study of the Constitution and proposed about 50 changes, which were subsequently approved. Some of the more important changes made to update the document at that time were as follows: broadening the list of commodities and research problems to include those of concern in public health as well as agriculture; naming other national agencies besides USDA as organizations whose chemists may become active members; permitting qualified scientists in municipal laboratories to become active members by application and approval; allowing individuals who serve AOAC as Associate Referees or liaison officers to be recognized as Associate Members, even if they are otherwise ineligible; and permitting only one vote from each state or province on general questions. The major effect of the changes, since the Bylaws had gotten out of date, was to bring them into conformity with ongoing procedures and clarify them. The committee recommended that it serve one more year, but it has become a permanent standing committee, adding changes to the Bylaws as they are necessitated by Association actions. The terms "Constitution" and "Bylaws" had been used interchangeably since the earliest existence of AOAC. In 1975, the Committee on the Constitution formally changed the title to Bylaws when it rearranged and clarified the entire document. Extensive activity by this committee also was necessary to incorporate the appropriate bylaw revisions when AOAC became "independent" of the Food and Drug Administration in the early 1970s.

Committee on Statistics

The Committee on Statistics was initiated in 1962, and that year AOAC sponsored a special evening lecture at the annual meeting by Dr. W. J. Youden, who discussed how statistical interpretation could be of value in designing collaborative tests. Dr. Youden subsequently was asked to prepare a set of statistical guidelines for AOAC with the cooperation of the committee. In 1968, the committee recommended minimal collaborative test requirements for adoption of analytical methods and published them as part of the annual report. It also agreed to conduct a session for the General Referees one evening during each annual meeting on the general topic of accuracy and precision. Under the auspices of the Statistics Committee, the Association was moving rapidly into the full utilization of statistics to design and evaluate its collaborative studies.

In 1974, a consulting statistician was assigned to each subcommittee on methods to lend statistical assistance for adopting valid and reliable methods. The statistician was given the duty of reviewing the experimental design before the beginning of a collaborative study, and also of reviewing the validity and form of the statistical analysis for the Associate Referee reports recommending a method for first action status. This person does not have a vote on the Committee on Official Methods, but does present opinions on whether the recommendation is statistically sound and and in agreement with results as presented. This arrangement has proved eminently satisfactory.

In 1980, the suggestion was put forward that the Committee on Statistics might be combined with the Committee on Collaborative Studies to handle the interrelated problems more effectively, but the former felt it would be desirable to retain the present form and interact with other pertinent committees when indicated. The placement of volunteers from the Statistics Committee on subcommittees of the Collaborative Studies Committee provided a good mechanism for such interaction.

Joint Mycotoxins Committee

Throughout its existence, the Association has had numerous joint committees in cooperation with various other organizations interested in analytical methodology. Most of these committees have been of relatively short duration; long term cooperation has been maintained through the activities of liaison representatives coordinating AOAC activities with those of other groups. However, the Joint Mycotoxins Committee has been in existence and expanding its activities since 1965. It was originally organized at that time as the Joint AOCS-AOAC Committee on Aflatoxins in cooperation with the American Oil Chemists Society (AOCS). The importance of aflatoxins as impurities in feeds and other edible products was gaining recognition, and a General Referee was appointed by AOAC in 1965. The Joint AOCS-AOAC Committee was created to evaluate and recommend reliable, practical uniform methods which would not differ among the interested groups of analysts.

In 1969, the committee's responsibility was expanded to include mycotoxins as a group, and the name was revised to reflect that change. In 1970, with the addition of representatives of the American Association of Cereal Chemists (AACC), who also had similar interests in mycotoxin methodology, the group became the Joint AOAC-AOCS-AACC Mycotoxin Committee. The most recent addition to the organizations represented on the Joint Mycotoxin Committee has been the International Union of Pure and Applied Chemistry (IUPAC). The present objectives of the joint committee, stated in their 1980 report, are to coordinate the development of mycotoxin methods in the four societies involved, to establish the priorities for methods development, and to establish general guidelines for collaborative studies of mycotoxin methods. Thus it serves an important function in controlling the proliferation of standard methods. As a consequence of its annual meetings, it has also been able to serve in disseminating information on many aspects of mycotoxin research. In addition to reporting on all phases of mycotoxin poisoning episodes and high-mycotoxin incidents, the committee also serves to publicize meetings and symposia concerned with the subject.

Committee on Safety

A general growing awareness of the importance of laboratory safety, particularly from the standpoint of possible contact of personnel with toxic or carcinogenic reagents, prompted the Executive Committee in 1965 to request that the president appoint a committee to study the desirability of including safety principles in *Official Methods of Analysis*. The committee's first major accomplishment was the preparation of a new chapter on safety for the eleventh edition of *Official Methods of Analysis*. They also prepared a list of those methods proposed for the Book of Methods which they deemed to need some sort of cautionary statement for the analyst. Revision and updating of the chapter on laboratory safety has been one of the principal functions of the committee since that time.

One of the earliest concerns was the recovery of mercury from residues remaining after the Kjeldahl distillation in the official method. Residues had always been disposed of in the sink. Recommendations for revision of the published method were made to eliminate the hazard. The Committee on Safety has also monitored official government and international agency declarations on carcinogenic reagents and advised the Association when alternative methods should be sought to eliminate their use. Disposal methods for hazardous reagents or residues have also been developed or recommended, and the committee has continuously reviewed the lists of reagents of AOAC methods to determine if there is an indicated need for special precautions in handling or disposing of them which is not mentioned in the text. The 1974 report of the committee invited comments and suggestions from user/analysts concerning possible safety problems encountered. As a result, the committee has received communications pointing out practical problems which might otherwise not have been recognized. Members of the Committee on Safety have volunteered to make themselves available for advice to individual members. This is especially helpful in matters of disposal of hazardous materials.

The committee was requested to conduct a symposium on laboratory safety at the 1980 annual meeting. The very successful Laboratory Safety Symposium attracted a standing-room-only audience. This conscientious committee has presented a formal report each year and now supplements its report with notices in *The Referee* when appropriate.

Committee on International Cooperation

Even though the official designation of AOAC contained the restriction "of North America" for many years, the Association began cooperation with its foreign counterparts long before the Committee on International Cooperation was established in 1968 as recommended by the Long Range Planning Committee.

The Committee on International Cooperation was formed to coordinate AOAC activities with similar or related activities outside North America, and arrange for cooperation in development, testing, and adoption of analytical methods. This committee brought into focus a trend toward AOAC's becoming an international organization. This trend had been developing for many years and had gained momentum rapidly since the inception of the Committee on Improvement.

As early as the tenth annual convention in 1893, a resolution was passed directing Secretary Harvey Wiley to communicate with the leading chemists and chemical associations of foreign countries to apprise them of the work currently being pursued by AOAC, and to invite their participation in collaborative studies. Two hundred fifty letters were sent, offering test samples and copies of the methods under collaborative study to any volunteers who might come forth. This was the beginning of a successful effort to recruit foreign collaborators, many of whom were already using AOAC methods. The tenth meeting held in Chicago was the first held outside of Washington since the Association had been organized. The reason was that the World's Fair and the Columbian Scientific Exposition taking place there were expected to draw a large number of foreign agricultural scientists and, it was hoped, to provide an opportunity for interaction. Although there was always a desire for exchange of ideas and cooperation at the collaborator level, for a long period, AOAC proudly preserved its identity as a North American entity. At the 24th annual meeting in 1907, President J. P. Street insisted that the designation "of North America" be stipulated in the Constitution as part of the name of the Association, and that the Constitution be further amended to specify that Canada and Mexico be the only foreign countries entitled to representation.

Even though foreign scientists attended AOAC meetings from time to time, and AOAC members attended international meetings on occasion, there was little recognition of the value of formal cooperation until relatively recent times. Dr. C. R. Shabetai of the Permanent International Bureau of Analytical Chemistry in Paris, France, was an invited guest speaker at the 1957 meeting of AOAC. Then, in 1963, several actions were formally taken by the Executive Committee to draw the attention of international bodies to the work of the Association and to acknowledge the desirability of foreign cooperation. They approved a policy of authorizing appointment of Associate Referees from outside North America, provided that no one in North America was available to accept the problem and that the proposed Associate Referees would acquaint themselves with AOAC collaborative study requirements and would attend at least an occasional meeting. They also initiated plans to provide for invited foreign guests at the following year's meeting and asked the meeting committee to arrange the program to accommodate such visitors. Scientific associations were placed on the mailing list and invited to the meetings. The Executive Committee also approved, in principle, cooperation with the Collaborative Pesticide Analytical Committee in Europe (later CIPAC) and recommended certain provisions to assure that methods adopted by CIPAC would meet AOAC recommended standards. Finally, a Committee on Foreign Visitors was established to help expedite the arrangements for the invited guests.

The program of bringing foreign visitors to the 1965 meeting was originally suggested by the Long Range Planning Committee and was made possible with funding support from the Division of Environmental Engineering and Food Protection of the U.S. Public Health Service. Seven prestigious scientists from Denmark, England, France, and the Netherlands attended the meeting as honored guests and presented addresses describing various aspects of regulatory analysis in their own countries. Four foreign scientists, including one from Italy and one from Japan, accepted invitations to speak at the 1966 meeting, financed by a similar grant. The success of this undertaking did much to advance the program of international cooperation.

AOAC was beginning to investigate opportunities for liaison with other groups, such as CIPAC. In response to a Long Range Planning Committee suggestion in 1968, the Executive Committee established the Committee on International Cooperation to advise and keep AOAC aware of relevant activities in domestic and foreign organizations. The responsibilities have expanded in the intervening years until, at present, the Committee also has the following function, as stated in the AOAC handbook: "Informs AOAC of similar activities in other organizations outside the United States and provides, devises, promotes, and facilitates working arrangements with other groups; recommends policy and procedures concerning adoption of methods from other organizations; encourages other organizations to adopt collaborative study principles and use methods determined to be reliable."

In his 1968 presidential speech, Bruce Poundstone stated that "perhaps the greatest challenge to AOAC is the cooperative development of completely compatible methods of analysis for international use." He discussed the state of cooperation at that time, including participation in the activities of CIPAC, the International Association for Cereal Chemistry, the International Dairy Federation, the International Standards Organization, and the Pesticide Analysis Committee of the Ministry of Agriculture of the United Kingdom (PAC). The Committee on International Cooperation provided a vehicle for coordinating this rapidly expanding area of AOAC activity.

The first report of the committee, made in 1968, reviewed the relationships which AOAC already had with international organizations and noted that AOAC had liaison representatives to a number of national and international associations. A good beginning had been made toward international cooperation in the study of a limited number of analytical methods. The committee felt that recent work on the development of methods in North America had emphasized work on analysis of substances from a health hazard viewpoint. Those substances included pesticide residues, food and feed additives, packaging materials, microorganisms, and mycotoxins. At the same time, the committee recognized that analysts in other areas of the world had been developing methods for the analysis of food composition which could be very useful to AOAC in keeping such methods up to date and applicable in world trade.

Regarding relationships and procedures, the committee felt that initially relationships with other associations should be flexible, since they would vary depending on the nature and extent of mutual interest, and on individual organizational circumstances. The report also recommended a policy regarding adoption and use by AOAC of methods resulting from international cooperation. At least one collaborator should be a reputable analyst from North America if a satisfactorily conducted study was to be adopted by AOAC. However, exceptions could be made for methods extensively studied overseas.

Perhaps the most significant initial recommendation proposed by the Committee on International Cooperation to the Executive Committee was that a symposium on international methods be held during the annual regular meeting two years later, in the fall of 1970. The purpose of the symposium was to inform the general AOAC membership of the work of other international and national organizations outside North America involved in the development and testing of analytical methods. The symposium proposal was, again, presented to the Executive Committee in 1969 and accepted.

In 1969 the Committee on International Cooperation prepared a list of about 100 international organizations with an interest in the development of methods of analysis, and selected four with which to begin a detailed study of the methods developed, together with the procedures used in their development. These four were the Nordic Committee on Food Analysis, the Analytical Methods Committee of the Society of Analytical Chemistry of the United Kingdom, the International Union of Pure and Applied Chemistry, and the International Standards Organization and its various technical committees. The activities of some of these groups were already familiar to the Association from previous presentations by foreign guest speakers. Presentations by some of the speakers at the Symposium on the Development of Methods of Analysis by International Organizations, held at the annual AOAC meeting in October of 1970 served to acquaint the AOAC membership with the operations of the other groups. The highly successful symposium brought to the attention of the AOAC membership at large the international involvement of the Association, and presented a forum for the assembled representatives of various international scientific organizations to discuss interactions with AOAC.

This committee has energetically pursued a course of active exchange of ideas with counterpart organizations, enlarging the areas for cooperation each year. In 1971, it was proposed that a tabulation of methods be made to compare international methods with similar AOAC procedures, so they could be referred to the methods subcommittees for possible joint collaborative testing. Unfortunately, it was not possible to carry out this plan, although a series of formal liaisons with various international organizations was inaugurated. In 1973, AOAC was granted associate organizational status with the International Union of Pure and Applied Chemistry. A successful meeting of CIPAC and a joint symposium with AOAC were held in conjunction with the 1971 annual AOAC meeting. Guidelines formalizing the ongoing cooperation between AOAC and CIPAC were ratified in 1974. Cooperative arrangements were also worked out with the International Committee on Microbiological Specifications, the Nordic Methods Committee on Food Analysis (NMKL), and the Office International du Cacao et du Chocolat (OICC). The principles of cooperation between the Analytical Methods Committee of the Society of Analytical Chemists and AOAC were finalized about 1975, shortly before SAC became the Analytical Division of the Chemical Society.

In 1971, AOAC observers attended the meeting of Technical Committee 34 (TC 34) of the International Standards Organization (ISO) dealing with agricultural food products, and in 1973 AOAC requested Type A observer status with certain ISO/TC 34 Committees. Participation in ISO Technical Committee 34 was important in terms of assisting in the establishment of uniform international methods of analysis of foods, particularly methodology for use by the joint FAO/WHO Codex Alimentarius program. Because of the interest of U.S. regulatory agencies, particularly for meat and poultry products, in the international activities of ISO, the Association subsequently became a member of the American National Standards Institute (ANSI), which is the private national standards organization representing the United States in ISO. The ANSI vote in matters pertaining to the Agricultural Food Products Technical Committee which functions through 15 subcommittees including meat, dairy, cereals, oils, fruits, vegetables, feeds was delegated, subject to certain conditions, to AOAC. Decisions regarding coffee and tea are handled by the trade associations for these products. This action provided an alternative entry into the consideration of methods for food products for the Codex Alimentarius for the United States, in addition to its direct access to the Codex mechanism. A recent development in this area is the 1980 endorsement by the ISO technical committee of the policy that all methods intended for submission to the Codex Alimentarius be collaboratively studied, a general policy long advocated by AOAC representatives.

Under the auspices of the Committee on International Cooperation, the policy of discussion of matters of common interest with other international groups, and the policy of Association member participation in international and national meetings both formally and as observers has continually been of considerable benefit to all concerned. There has been excellent representation from overseas at all the meetings of the committee and cooperation has been maintained at a high level. One accomplishment was the proposed beginning of publication in 1975 of the results of collaborative studies done by members of the Nordic Committee on Food Analysis. This had been previously prohibited by that group's bylaws, and the newly available data, if published, promised to be of value to AOAC.

In 1980, the membership of the committee was enlarged to formally include the Association of Public Analysts, which represents chemists directly involved in analytical activities in the United Kingdom. Their representatives had been frequent participants in the meetings.

The committee continues to maintain a high level of cooperation, with its activities supplemented by the efforts of the Association's European representative. J. P. van Ginckel was the first to hold this post, beginning in 1972. This was established as a regular part-time staff position in 1975 with the appointment of Margreet Tuinstra-Lauwaars of the Netherlands. The duties of the representative included presenting AOAC's comments at meetings of the working groups and committees of international organizations which work with AOAC at the technical level; expressing AOAC basic policy for development of internationally acceptable methods at such meetings;

indicating related method development work in progress in AOAC relevant to problems presented at the meetings; and providing international organizations with basic information about AOAC philosophy and procedures. The duties have been expanded to include talks and personal contacts in the interest of increasing the numbers of AOAC members, sustaining members, and Associate Referees in Europe by explaining the aims and function of the Association. This position has been an important segment of the AOAC international program.

Committee on Interlaboratory Studies

The present Committee, established in 1977 as the Committee on Collaborative Studies, provides guidelines for use by Associate Referees and others in designing, conducting, and interpreting collaborative studies. It was formed initially to answer questions posed by the former Committee on Classification of Methods in its 1977 report in regard to the specific requirements for acceptable collaborative studies, and by a general need for harmonization of international collaborative studies. Its subject matter and function were closely interrelated with those of the Committee on Classification of Methods, which was first appointed in 1973 to consider the question of the adoption of more than one method for the same constituent. It was also asked to consider the problem of adoption of screening methods. A prolonged effort on the part of this committee was undertaken to resolve the questions of screening methods and methods involving proprietary equipment, and to counter the criticism of slow adoption of methods and of duplication. The only official addition in the Bylaws to the existing official first action and official final action categories has been interim official first action. This applies to methods accepted by the Associate Referee, General Referee, and Methods Committee during the year, but not yet voted on at an annual meeting by the Association. To help resolve the interrelated problems of collaborative studies, methods classification, and automated methods, the two committees filed a joint report at the 1979 meeting to coordinate recommendations. This report focused on producing a uniform declaration of policy for AOAC, reflecting the concept that its purpose is to furnish methods of analysis accompanied by sufficient performance data to illustrate the reliability which can be expected. The policy stated that the AOAC should not put itself in the position of making administrative decisions on how and when any of its official methods should be used. Since different laboratories might use the same methods for different purposes, the decisions should be made by the user organization, based on published performance data in *Official Methods of Analysis*.

Consequently, the committees decided to suggest "Guidelines for Providing Performance Data for an AOAC Method" to be used to provide the performance data to accompany each new method in *Official Methods of Analysis*, beginning with the fourteenth edition.

This joint report was accepted by the Association and by the Board of Directors, which then charged the committee to reorganize and begin developing a protocol for the design and evaluation of collaborative studies in an attempt to meet the objectives outlined in the report. The charge to the committee included the following: "Provide guidelines for the design, conduct, and interpretation of collaborative studies and for review by the Committee on Official Methods; work with the Editorial Board in implementing the new policy; recommend studies to develop policies for the statistical selection of samples, and for the physical removal and handling of samples." In 1981, the reorganized Committee on Interlaboratory Studies accepted the difficult and complex charge and set up eight subcommittees as follows: definitions, design and conduct of collaborative studies, guidelines for statistical analysis, guidelines for performance of methods, guidelines for systems control of collaborative studies, sampling and sample preparation, reporting forms and data bases, and applications to biological tests. The committee and various subcommittees began their tasks immediately and preliminary progress reports were announced and released periodically as they became available. The target date for the final report was set for the 1984 Centennial Meeting.

The committee has also taken an active role in international harmonization of collaborative studies, a topic of great importance to AOAC in its increasing role as an international leader in method validation techniques. AOAC representatives have participated in symposia on harmonization held in Helsinki in 1981. An international symposium on harmonization is being held in conjunction with the AOAC centennial program in cooperation with IUPAC.

Committee on Laboratory Quality Assurance

Several events in the late 1970s led to the rejection of laboratory data in toxicological investigations that had been used to prove safety or efficacy of regulated commodities. Investigation indicated improper laboratory records and lack of quality assurance procedures, which cast suspicion on results from some laboratories.

With the growing recognition of the importance of laboratory quality assurance to any valid analytical program, AOAC organized a Committee on Laboratory Quality Assurance in 1980. The committee was formed to advise and recommend to the Board of Directors principles for application of quality assurance techniques to improve operations of analytical laboratories. The committee developed a plan to achieve this general goal, which included the preparation and publication by AOAC of a quality assurance manual for analytical laboratories. Existing or planned government and industry manuals and programs were identified and obtained for examination, when possible. In addition, the committee devised plans to encourage analytical laboratories to improve operations by adopting and applying quality assurance principles. A plan was also developed to encourage the use of quality control principles in AOAC methodology and by General Referees, Associate Referees, and others presenting reports at AOAC meetings. The committee also volunteered to assist the AOAC staff, on request, in reviewing and commenting on regulations proposed by federal, state, or provincial agencies which involve quality assurance principles or good laboratory practices. AOAC is well on the way to becoming a leader in promoting quality assurance techniques for laboratories.

Committee on Symposia and Special Programs

A committee on symposia was first mentioned in 1963 when the Executive Committee authorized the president to appoint a committee to consider future symposia. However, the committee was never officially appointed, perhaps because of the foreign visitor program scheduled for 1964 which required that the program be structured to accommodate those visitors. Even at this time, conducting symposia was not a new idea for AOAC. As early as the forty-seventh meeting in 1931, the program of the annual meeting included a Symposium on Analytical Methods. A similar symposium was presented for each of the next two years. Each was composed of a variety of presentations on subjects of interest to the Association with no focus on any specific problem. In 1953, the first symposium directed at a specific problem was presented: Symposium on Extraneous Materials in Foods and Drugs. In 1956, a Symposium on Pesticide Residue Methods for Fumigants was part of the annual meeting program, followed in 1957 by a Symposium on Microscopic Analytical Methods in the Food and Drug Industries, and in 1958 by one on Chick Edema Disease; the latter was identified as a polychlorinated dibenzeno dioxin problem, one of the earliest appearances of these extremely toxic compounds. The early symposia, like the present ones, responded to problems of important and practical significance to the Association and to the analytical community in general. They also served to bring new developments and techniques to the attention of the membership and the readers of the Journal by providing them with state-of-the-art reviews of timely analytical subjects.

Symposia were presented again in the early 1960s, but scheduling was not consistent, possibly because there were not always recognizable problems requiring such treatment. However, beginning in 1969 with a symposium on Drug Residues in Animal Tissues, a continuously expanding program of symposia at annual meetings was begun. From 1970 on, at least two and as many as six symposia have been presented at each. They have covered almost every aspect of analytical interest, including computers in the laboratory. The historical development of analytical chemistry during this period is reflected in the symposia titles.

Many of the symposia have been published in the Journal; in some instances, they have been published as separate pamphlets for general sale.

In 1981 a formal standing Committee on Symposia and Special Programs was formed to select topics and organizers of symposia for the annual meeting and to advise on short courses and other aspects of the scientific program. This committee may also advise on scope of the AOAC spring training workshops.

Committee on Performance of Instrumental Methods and Data Handling

Like several committees, the Committee on Performance of Instrumental Methods and Data Handling, formed in 1981, had its roots in other committees previously established to handle simpler versions of a more general problem. Its principal predecessor, the Committee on Automated Methods, was established 15 years earlier when it was evident that the systems of instruments being used to fully automate wet chemical methods were ushering in a new era in analytical chemistry. Because the manufacturers claimed, convincingly, that any spectrophotometric, flame photometric, fluorometric, or nephelometric method could be automated, and because over half the AOAC methods involved such determinative steps, there was pressure on Associate Referees to include automation in their methodologies. Papers on automation of phosphorus and potassium methods had already been presented at the annual meeting by 1966. The Committee on Automated Methods was appointed to study the problems which might arise and recommend a policy for handling this type of method.

Since the problem was a general one, the committee consulted with other analytical organizations. They found that only the American Oil Chemists' Society and the American Society for Testing and Materials had considered the topic. Both had decided to require collaborative test proof that the reproducibility and accuracy of their accepted standard methods would not be adversely affected by incorporation of automation steps. The committee recommended that the AOAC follow the same policy, especially since it maintained liaison with both organizations.

The committee continued its activity in this area for the next 15 years. It requested that referees survey their subjects for possible automation of either a whole procedure or a single step. By 1969, some collaborative studies were under way. New Associate Referees were being appointed to study various automated methods and by the 1970 meeting three automated methods were recommended for official first action. An outline of steps for describing automated methods was incorporated into the style manual.

Meanwhile, the committee began to obtain a list of laboratories that had automated equipment available. By 1970, this list had grown to about 70 laboratories and was very useful in locating new Associate Referees and prospective collaborators. Since more and more papers on the subject were being presented, a Symposium on Automated Methods and Computer-Assisted Analysis was proposed and presented in 1973. One prediction made at that time was that within a few years all instruments would include a computer as an integral part. We have come very close to seeing that as a reality.

With ten automated methods appearing in the twelfth edition of *Official Methods of Analysis*, in 1974, the committee put forth guidelines for future collaborative studies of automated methods. In 1977, the committee established a set of terms for identification of the various degrees of method automation. It also developed guidelines for changes in official automated methods which would not require that a full collaborative study be done. These guidelines were accepted, and an edited version was approved by the Board of Directors for inclusion in the AOAC handbook. The committee also endorsed the joint report of the Committee on Collaborative Studies and the Committee on Classification of Methods in 1979, citing it as a framework within which its own objectives could be achieved.

In its final report in 1980, the Committee on Automated Methods recommended that a special commitee be appointed to develop generic rather than manufacturer-specific instrument specifications and that a chapter be included in *Official Methods of Analysis* dealing with performance specifications of instruments commonly used in official methods. They also proposed that a special committee be designated to consider policy recommendations concerning computers and microprocessers in the laboratory.

An existing committee of the same nature was the Committee on Gas Chromatography of Pesticide Formulations which had been appointed in 1973 and had given its only report in 1975. In that report it had set down an excellent and extensive set of guidelines and recommendations for the use of gas chromatography for regulatory purposes in the pesticide area. The Executive Committee recommended in 1975 that instrumental methods adopted by AOAC must meet certain reliability criteria, that details must be printed when feasible, and that, preferably, the Associate Referee should not be a representative of the instrument manufacturer. In 1981, noting the proposals in the final report of the Committee on Automated Methods, the Board of Directors combined this committee with the Committee on Gas and Liquid Chromatography under the new designation, Committee on Performance of Instrumental Methods and Data Handling. The new committee was charged with the development of specifications for instrumentation and performance. It was also directed to plan a symposium in this area for the 1983 annual meeting. The orderly integration of automation into official methods to take advantage of its enormous potential has been a challenge to the Association. However, the Association has kept pace with the advancing technology through the excellent work of its committees.

Independence in the Seventies

Funding for the operation of AOAC had traditionally come from two main sources, the sale of *Official Methods of Analysis* and support from United States government agencies, chiefly the U.S. Department of Agriculture and the Food and Drug Administration. The initial support in the USDA Bureau of Chemistry under Wiley's aegis was primarily on an informal basis, but funds were later designated for AOAC in the federal budgets from 1903 to 1907. Then the budget item did not appear again until 1919, although support from the government was maintained during the interim. From that time until 1944, the budget item appeared annually. In 1944 the Appropriation Act provided authority for FDA to expend funds for organizations dealing with the development of methods as a permanent, continuing expense, and FDA remained constant in its generous support of the Association, especially by providing able personnel and office space.

This relationship was questioned in 1970 in a report to Dr. Charles Edwards, the Commissioner of Food and Drugs, by a committee he had appointed to critically review the operations of various units and activities of FDA and make suggestions for change where indicated. The committee was known as the FDA Ad Hoc Science Advisory Committee, or Ritts Committee after its chairman. As a consequence of this report, AOAC was obliged to embark on a course which drastically altered the Association's management, operation, scope of interest and activity, and means of support. It heralded the reorganization of AOAC into a truly self-supporting, independent, professional association without sacrificing the integrity of its major function, namely the development, testing, and adoption of official methods of analysis in the interest of regulatory and research organizations in agriculture and public health. The committee lauded AOAC and its activities, stating, in part, "The Association of Official Analytical Chemists occupies a time-honored and a significant role in developing analytical procedures, which are, like those certified by the United States Pharmacopeia, generally accepted as official. The value of AOAC to FDA is the fact that the mere listing of an analytical method in the AOAC syllabus is the imprimatur that ordinarily gives the method validity and acceptance by both sides in litigations before the federal courts." It then went on to point out that FDA was a strong supporter of AOAC and had become both the major producer and major user of the validated analytical methods, with over half the associate refereeships held by FDA personnel. The report then discussed the problems it felt to be inherent in the relationship:

"While the leaders and staff of AOAC are, in the Committee's opinion, men and women of competence, integrity, and high purpose, the Committee must look at the present relationship between AOAC and FDA with a degree of concern, more for its appearance than for what it actually is. As in issues of conflict, where the appearance can be as damaging as the actual guilt, there are facets of the AOAC-FDA relationship, which in the hands of the poorly motivated, could embarrass FDA. As examples, certain FDA employees whose titles, grades, and job description indicate otherwise actually spend significant portions of their official working time on AOAC business, in the capacity of AOAC officials; at times one can be easily confused as to when they operate as AOAC officials and when as FDA employees. Government space in FDA Building FB-8, as well as supplies and facilities, are utilized to a significant extent for AOAC business. The law requires that the AOAC use a different mail address (The Benjamin Franklin Station) than the actual working address of most of its officers (200 C Street, SW, Washington, DC) even though the residence of AOAC in FDA is common knowledge. These facts give the appearance of subterfuge and an interlocking directorate. Furthermore, by the awarding of refereeships and methods development projects to applicant District laboratories, sometimes in competition with each other, the awarding AOAC official who is also a FDA staff member appears to play the role of assigning FDA science priorities and research time, when such functions are not included among (that person's) FDA job responsibilities.

"The Committee recognizes the importance of AOAC to FDA and to other regulatory agencies of the federal and state governments. The Committee is also appreciative of the hard work, dedication, and competence of its members and officials. For these reasons, the Committee believes that AOAC and its staff should no longer be subjected to operating under its current unsatisfactory administrative arrangement. The Committee recommends that FDA play a major role in obtaining full and acknowledged support of AOAC so that it can operate as an independent scientific society with quarters in the private sector, staffed by salaried personnel, supplied through regular private commercial sources, and led by volunteer and/or paid professionals as the governing board of the Association may decide. Such support might be provided by an FDA grant or contract, and other federal agencies might be solicited for their willingness to provide similar subsidies. It might be even more appropriate for the Department of Health, Education and Welfare, or the Public Health Service to be the sponsoring agency. Whatever mechanism is worked out should permit AOAC to continue its important mission for FDA and other federal and state agencies but

also enable it to be independent, open, and supported appropriately as
the prestigious, official methods-validating body it is."

Shortly after the report was submitted to Commissioner Edwards, he wrote
to AOAC President Henry Davis notifying him that the Commissioner
concurred in the recommendation "that steps be taken to obtain full and
acknowledged support of your organization so that it can operate as an
independent scientific society." Edwards suggested that a task force be
appointed from AOAC membership with representation from among the
various agencies benefiting from AOAC activities. He further suggested that
a plan be ready for submission in six months, reiterating that AOAC was
important to FDA and other agencies of the federal and state governments.
A task force had originally been requested by AOAC Executive Director
William Horwitz in a memorandum commenting on the ad hoc report in
which he eloquently defended the situation of FDA-AOAC cooperation as it
existed. Donald Mitchell, AOAC Vice President, also wrote to Edwards in
behalf of the Executive Committee, pointing out that the Ritts Committee
had raised no scientific question regarding the relationship between AOAC
and FDA. He suggested that perhaps minor changes in the AOAC constitution and in job descriptions could solve the "appearance of conflict of
interest" issue. He pointed out that the administrative and legal questions
of conflict of interest raised by the Ritts Committee had been repeatedly
investigated by administrative officers, personnel officers, and legal authorities from the U.S. Departments of Agriculture and Health, Education and
Welfare, and also by the General Accounting Office and General Services
Administration. In all instances, these bodies endorsed continued support of
AOAC by FDA.

The Association did acquiesce, however, in Edwards' request for a task
force to develop a proposal for continued support, and suggested that it
consist of one representative from each of the major agencies contributing to
and utilizing the services of the AOAC. They were the Food and Drug
Administration; Environmental Protection Agency; U.S. Department of
Agriculture; Bureau of Narcotics and Dangerous Drugs; Department of
Justice; Alcohol, Tobacco and Firearms Division of the Internal Revenue
Service; Canadian Food and Drug Directorate; Canadian Department of
Agriculture; state regulatory agencies, state universities, and industry (rep-
resentative as an observer).

Commissioner Edwards had originally preferred that the actual investigation and proposal be handled through an outside contract, but dropped
the idea as less desirable and less economical when he received the AOAC
proposal that the task force consist of representatives of the various agencies.

He wrote to Vice President Mitchell on November 10, 1971, "I am therefore asking that the charge to the AOAC Task Force be expanded to include the study, report, and recommendation, rather than the earlier limitation to develop the scope of a contract and the criteria for a contractor. The constructive alternative suggestions outlined in your letter of October 22, 1971, should be brought to the attention of the Task Force as well as the suggestions of the Ad Hoc Science Advisory Committee. It may well be these alternatives proposed by AOAC, such as changes in the Constitution and selection of Associate Referees, may be adequate to overcome the concerns expressed. If not, some combination of these alternatives and the approaches suggested by the Ad Hoc Science Advisory Committee may be adequate for full support of AOAC." Edwards also assured Mitchell that FDA desired to maintain a strong and effective AOAC, capable of independent operation in the validation and adoption of methods, since this was essential to the mission of FDA.

The Interagency Task Force was duly appointed and met on December 15, 1971. The results of their deliberations were submitted to Dr. Edwards on January 31, 1972, on schedule with the time-table he had requested. In his letter, Vice President Mitchell related that the consensus of the Task Force was that the existing AOAC-FDA relationship was highly desirable and beneficial to all concerned and should be continued with some modifications in AOAC's operations. He then listed, with comments, the recommendations they had formulated for revisions in the AOAC Constitution and procedures which should eliminate the basis for the charge of an appearance of conflict of interest. It was also proposed that the subject of possible support from other agencies be explored. The letter further stated that, unless advised to the contrary, a meeting of the Executive Committee of AOAC would be called to pass on the submission of the constitutional revisions to the membership at the annual meeting in October 1972 and to institute the suggested changes in operating policies immediately. Two weeks later, Commissioner Edwards replied to the report in a very positive manner, stating that he agreed that the recommendations of the Task Force were responsive to the suggestions made by the Ritts Committee and promising continued support from the Food and Drug Administration. He requested that he be kept informed on the final action taken on the proposed constitutional amendments and on the progress made in obtaining financial support from other agencies.

The constitutional and operational changes were revised and accepted by the Executive Committee on June 2, 1972, and were approved at the annual meeting in October 1972. They provided for changes in AOAC procedure, but did not affect the collaborative study process or the integrity of method adoption. In fact, the new constitutional changes guaranteed the autonomy and independent authority of the Committee on Official Methods in all matters concerning scientific choice, validation, and adoption of methods by AOAC. Changes in the Constitution provided that no methods subcommittee (now committee) could be staffed with a majority of members of a single agency and that the name of the Committee on Recommendations of Referees be changed to the Committee on Official Methods. The reason for the latter change was to avoid any inference that this committee appointed the referees and to reflect its true function: to recommend adoption or rejection of methods. A provision was also added to the Constitution requiring that the appointment of Associate Referees from within government agencies must have the approval of their appropriate supervisors. This was to assure that government employees acting in their capacity as AOAC officials would not be in a position to appoint other government employees, not under their supervision, to Associate Refereeships. Appointment letters of Associate and General Referees employed by a government agency must state that organizational approval had been obtained, and when it was not clear to the Associate Referee or General Referee which method should be collaborated, they should seek the advice of their Methods Committee, which might wish to recommend the use of a group of experts to decide the best method to study. To overcome the Ritts Committee criticism of the use of a post office box address instead of the address of FDA, AOAC began using the actual address of offices on the Journal and other appropriate documents.

Appointment of FDA employees as officials of AOAC was not considered by the Task Force to be a legitimate problem and they did not recommend that this situation be changed. Commissioner Edwards agreed with this viewpoint. In replying to the letter from then President Mitchell who had written him in November 1972 to advise him of the constitutional and operational changes which had been made, Edwards wrote, "I agree with your statement that as a matter of policy those in policy and operational positions in AOAC should be government officials and not AOAC employees. Further, I agree that FDA should support certain AOAC-related positions as it has done in the past." He also acknowledged that AOAC had satisfactorily answered the questions raised by the Ritts Committee and commended it for the seriousness with which the Association undertook the assignment and the successful results achieved.

Another recommendation of the Task Force was that the Office of the Executive Director of AOAC assemble information on fiscal and program requirements of AOAC and on the extent of participation and use of AOAC methods by various government agencies. The purpose was to enable individual members of the Task Force to discuss the possibility of financial support for AOAC in their own agencies. Such support could be used either to provide for expansion of services or to allow for reduced FDA support. By November 1972, an annual renewable grant of $20,000 had been provided by the Canadian government and a new cooperative agreement with the Department of Agriculture's Animal and Plant Health Inspection Service for $15,000 annually had been consummated. The funds were designated by AOAC for use to hire additional professional staff to serve the needs of all regulatory agencies.

When the Executive Committee acted on the Task Force report, it recommended that the Task Force be disbanded and replaced by another interagency committee with representatives having authority to commit their agencies to long-term relationship with AOAC. This would enable AOAC to determine agency needs and establish various possible levels of activity, and to seek support accordingly. The new committee could have the same members or others representing the agencies involved.

The Canadian support was renewed in 1973 and became a regular budget item. USDA contracts were increased to $30,000 in 1973 and also have continued on a yearly basis. Several state regulatory agencies began supporting AOAC with contractual agreements similar to those negotiated with U.S. and Canadian federal agencies. New York, Indiana, Mississippi, and South Dakota were early entries into such state/AOAC agreements. Funds gradually increased to supplement the FDA contribution, which was primarily in the form of personnel, space, and equipment, but which was by far the major AOAC source of support exclusive of publications income. The chief FDA relationship with the Association continued to reside in the Bureau of Foods, which provided the highly skilled personnel for AOAC-related activities.

Many members of AOAC, and particularly those on the Executive Committee and the Long Range Planning Committee, recognized that although this was a very crucial period for the Association it was also a time of great opportunity. In the early part of 1973, the Long Range Planning Committee began to evaluate the objectives and goals of the Association, with the intention of then establishing a stepwise program for their accomplishment. Ad hoc subcommittees were formed for such things as publication policies, development of methods review, modernization of the Constitution, extension of AOAC into service areas, and broadening the role of AOAC. The work of these subcommittees and others, which continued for several years, led to significant advances in each of these areas in the next decade. These included important changes in publicizing AOAC and its accomplishments, drastic changes in membership categories and privileges, and many new activities and liaisons for the organization. A new staff position was established, providing for a scientist/administrator paid from Association funds to assist in daily management of AOAC.

The feeling of the membership at this period was perhaps best expressed by the title of Mr. Garfield's presidential address at the beginning of the 1974 annual meeting: "The AOAC - Where Do We Go From Here." After reviewing the events that had transpired since the Ritts Committee Report, Garfield concluded: "What AOAC needs is a new long range philosophy appreciative of the needs of members and of new ways of thought, and new and imaginative management which recognizes that risk taking is a natural accompaniment of progress. The Association must develop competence in depth and it must place younger members on committees. It must continue to maintain high principles and standards, but if it fails to generate drive and effectiveness and to adjust to changes in the external environment it will become a stodgy rather than an enlightened and vibrant organization. It is a common axiom in business that planning and review are part and parcel of the entire organization. Therefore, there must be input and participation by each and every member. Where AOAC goes from here is up to the members. I hope they will decide to help us administer the AOAC with a sense of competitive urgency until we achieve the independent status we seek."

During the next year, the validity of this philosophy was borne out by further changes in the arrangements with the Food and Drug Administration. The responsibility for conducting its relationship with AOAC had been shifted from the Bureau of Foods to the Associate Commissioner for Science of FDA, Dr. L. B. Tepper. The reason given was that the AOAC-related activities were not food-specific, but related to virtually every area of FDA responsibility, as well as to the responsibilities of other government agencies and departments. FDA had already issued a statement of policy in the *Federal Register* in 1972 proclaiming the requirement to use AOAC methods in compliance programs unless otherwise stated. This welcome statement formally recognized the essentiality of AOAC procedures in the FDA compliance program. Now Dr. Tepper outlined several elements of basic policy to broaden and strengthen the FDA-AOAC relationship: (1) FDA was committed to preserving the integrity of AOAC as an independent, self-governing scientific organization; (2) FDA would continue to support AOAC at least to the same level as in the past as long as budget permitted; (3) FDA wished to avoid undue influence or domination of the Association in fact or appearance, and to that end it would encourage broad- based participation of other elements of the scientific community such as state governments, academia, industry, and other federal agencies and their counterpart organizations in other countries. At this time the primary sources of income for the operation of AOAC were the sale of *Official Methods of Analysis*, the "invisible" support from FDA in the form of personnel and services calculated to be about $150 000 per year, and the smaller contributions from other federal and state agencies and Canadian government agencies.

Shortly thereafter, the entire question of AOAC's future mode of operation was opened again when the Commissioner of Food and Drugs, Dr. A. M. Schmidt, informed AOAC President I. Hoffman that "a number of coinciding external forces" had caused FDA to carefully reconsider some of the problems raised in the 1971 Ritts Committee Report. He was specifically concerned with the fact that FDA, unlike other government agencies, made its contribution to staff and material resources for AOAC in a manner which was not visible or generally recognized, and consequently might be misconstrued as being secret or subversive to AOAC. He explained that he was actually aware of the importance of AOAC to the agency mission and that he did not want to jeopardize that relationship. For that reason, he proposed several immediate actions and others to be taken, preferably during the following 12 months, to correct the situation and provide complete openness regarding the arrangement. To resolve the situation, Mr. Garfield and Dr. Hoffman met with representatives of FDA and then with the rest of the AOAC Executive Committee. The resultant agreement provided that the FDA would publish a notice in the *Federal Register* and an article in the FDA popular periodical, *FDA Consumer*, in order to set forth clearly in the public record FDA's relationship with AOAC. The article was also to include details on past and present financial support of AOAC operations and to reaffirm FDA's commitment to support the Association both scientifically and financially. It also provided that each FDA annual report from then on would include a statement reflecting FDA's financial support of AOAC.

It was mandated that the support which was being provided by FDA in terms of space, services, and personnel would be replaced by a direct cash subsidy in the form of a protected or assured contract or grant. AOAC agreed to include details of the financial support received from all sources in its annual financial report published in the Journal. Where appropriate, the AOAC physical location was to be shown as the Food and Drug Administration Building at 200 C St, SW, Washington, DC, but to relieve FDA of the time-consuming burden of handling AOAC mail and to ensure efficient delivery, the post office box number format was retained on the letterhead. A realistic time frame was ageed on, two to five years, for the Association to develop and achieve the projected independent role. AOAC requested assurance that FDA officers who were then serving as AOAC key officials would be available during the transition period, and FDA acquiesced. A search committee was formed to develop a description and set of required qualifications for the paid position of chief executive officer to replace Horwitz and to suggest possible candidates. It was hoped that the position could be filled within a year, since the transition period was limited and the maximum possible period was desirable to permit Executive Director Horwitz and Executive Secretary Luther Ensminger to train the new executive officers in their respective functions and duties.

The Executive Committee continued to explore various options in order to increase AOAC's financial independence. The Long Range Planning Committee, which had endorsed the new agreement, prepared a letter and back-up material on "AOAC--What It Is and What It Does," which the Association issued and sent to commissioners of state departments of agriculture asking for financial support for AOAC. Several commitments of financial and moral support were obtained in response. The committee also formulated five and ten year plans for AOAC, including suitable time tables, development of financial needs, and ways and means to achieve independence.

Another innovation resulting from the implementation of the Ritts Committee recommendations was the establishment of the office of treasurer in 1974. The limited functions of the treasurer had traditionally been handled by the Executive Director or Secretary but it was felt that the actual and planned growth of the Association's activities and the increase in the Association's financial resources required the establishment of this separate elected office. The first elected treasurer, Bernhard Larsen of USDA, formulated a set of formal duties for the treasurer and also requested the formation of a 3-member finance committee with the treasurer as chairman. Both the excellent tabulation of duties and the suggested Finance Committee were approved by the Executive Committee. A major responsibility of the Finance Committee was to oversee the Association's investments to achieve maximum return consistent with fully safeguarded principal. The committee was also responsible for recommending a firm for each annual audit of the AOAC records. The financial practices and procedures of the Association were examined by a consultant firm, and various recommendations for improvement were suggested and initiated, such as the use of checks preprinted with serial numbers and providing automatic copies for accounting purposes. It also became quickly evident that a comptroller should be added to the staff and would be crucial to the organization that AOAC was rapidly becoming. Such a person would be especially needed for contracts.

Dr. Morton Beroza, who had retired from USDA, was appointed the first AOAC Contract Coordinator with authority to negotiate contracts directly with the federal agencies, subject only to final approval by the Executive Committee.

Mr. Garfield, who had previously retired from federal service, was engaged by AOAC in 1975 to develop a grant proposal seeking financial support from FDA, as part of the endeavor to develop independent administrative management of the Association in the shortest practical period of time.

Garfield immediately commenced discussions with FDA to explore the possible mode and extent of support AOAC might gain. He was an excellent choice for this job because he had served AOAC in many capacities including president, he was a highly experienced retired official who had served both FDA and the Drug Enforcement Agency, and he had great enthusiasm and optimism regarding the opportunities AOAC would have as an independently financed and controlled scientific society. In May 1976, the Executive Committee authorized Mr. Garfield to negotiate an agreement with FDA that would provide monetary support for the positions of Deputy Executive Director and managing editor and for secretarial assistance, as well as office space, supplies, and administrative services.

After considerable negotiation, the FDA/AOAC agreement was completed by Garfield in October 1976 and was signed by AOAC President Epps and FDA Commissioner Schmidt in the newly opened FDA Wiley Museum. This first direct financial support of AOAC by FDA was in the form of a memorandum of understanding. In the memorandum, FDA agreed to support AOAC for an interim period while AOAC agreed to begin to actively develop a broader financial base, to start transferring duties and functions from FDA employees to AOAC employees, and to search for private office space. The proposed deadline for complete transition was March 31, 1979. The search committee for the Deputy Executive Director, which had not been functioning pending the completion of the agreement, was reactivated, and Beroza and Garfield were continued as part-time consultants to generate government grants and contracts. The responsibilities of Mr. Garfied's position were enlarged to include working with other agencies.

The scope of AOAC activities was continuing to grow, with the technical review, publication, and distribution of three federal publications in 1971 and others in the succeeding years. The Consumer Product Safety Commission issued a purchase order for AOAC services to operate the methods validation program covering products under their jurisdiction. A slide series explaining the structure and activities of the AOAC was developed by Fred Bauer of Procter & Gamble Co. and Luther Ensminger, AOAC Executive Secretary. This series was shown at gatherings of government agencies and other associations to generate interest in AOAC affairs. Another innovation was the Spring Workshop and Training Conference, the first of which was held in Denver, Colorado, in May 1976. This highly successful gathering was attended by 330 persons who heard presentations on current analytical problems. After the third workshop, held in Atlanta in 1978, which attracted almost 500 persons, the Executive Committee approved the spring meeting as an annual event as long as attendance continued to cover costs. This workshop/conference, which now includes exhibits, has been held each year since then and has been a highly successful AOAC venture.

The Association had originally rejected the proposal suggested by FDA Commissioner Schmidt in 1975 that a moderate dues structure for individual AOAC members be imposed. At that time, the AOAC management felt that a membership dues structure was inappropriate because the actual membership was more institutional than personal in nature. However, in 1977 with the recommendation of the Long Range Planning Committee, a nominal $10 per year fee was instituted, with exemption from payment extended to those serving AOAC in an active capacity such as officer, committee member, or referee. Beginning in 1983, when the dues were increased to $25, the exemption ceased to be automatic, but was granted on request. The rationale for this consideration was that many of the volunteers who serve AOAC do so as part of their official work assignments and should not be expected to pay for this. While the dues structure has not yielded a significant amount of revenue as yet, it has served a very useful function in finally establishing a realistic individual membership body in keeping with the new organizational philosophy.

With the appointment of the new Deputy Executive Director in April 1977, AOAC was finally on the last lap to real administrative independence. Dr. David B. MacLean, who had been Director of Laboratory Services for the Minnesota Department of Agriculture, began a recommended training program with Dr. Horwitz and Mr. Ensminger on his arrival in September of 1977 and was approved to succeed Horwitz as Executive Director effective January 1, 1979. Mr. Ensminger retired as Executive Secretary at the same time. Also at that time, Mr. Garfield, who continued to be the chief liaison to FDA, was instructed by the Executive Committee to prepare a letter to the Commissioner of FDA stating that all appearances of conflict of interest between FDA and AOAC had been removed and that a statement of direct and indirect FDA support would be published annually as part of the Executive Director's report. The Executive Committee then authorized the positions of assistant to the Executive Director and comptroller to be advertised and filled by mid-1979 if possible. Since the management of government contracts was now an important consideration, the fiscal year was changed to October 1-September 30 to be in harmony with that of the U.S. federal government.

On April 28, 1979, the process of building an independent AOAC, begun eight years earlier, was completed when the staff moved its operations into new modern quarters in Arlington, Virginia, in an area readily accessible via the new Washington, DC, subway system. The financial base was steadily broadening with support then coming from seven federal agencies, 26 state agencies, and Health and Welfare Canada, but the financial stability was still far from being completely secure.

To aid in improving this situation, Eugene Holeman was appointed as the official liaison representative to the states, acting as goodwill ambassador and support solicitor. Holeman had already represented AOAC on occasion at such events as the Convention of State Commissioners of Agriculture, at which he had early been instrumental in getting the formal support, by resolution, of the newly independent Association. He visited many state officials and spoke at gatherings of state agricultural officers over several years. The support from this source was boosted very significantly through his efforts and those of others who campaigned for better state and provincial cooperation in financing AOAC.

Industry Participation

A major group which could contribute a great deal to the success of the Association, both from a financial viewpoint and in the form of participation and service, had been largely neglected by AOAC from its very beginnings. Participation by industry had been limited primarily to the activities of Associate Referees and participating collaborators by the fact that industial scientists were automatically designated Associate Members and governed by the restrictions of that membership category. Such restrictions might have had some merit in the past. Even before the official organization of the Association, there had been the experience of a method being adopted by majority vote of mostly nonofficial chemists, and then not used because the official chemists felt that it was not a valid procedure. But conditions had changed in almost 100 years and there was growing recognition that AOAC could better utilize available industrial resources. In his presidential address in 1978, A. J. Malanoski made a strong plea for the elimination of the existing distinctions between industry and official members, pointing out that the policy had been adopted when the AOAC had fewer than 75 members and industry in general had a much less enlightened attitude toward official methods. He cited the excellent cooperation of industry in developing and testing methods, and felt that industrial scientists were also qualified to participate in their adoption as official.

The Long Range Planning Committee was also concerned with the problem of industrial participation, and was considering the merits of expansion of this participation in all phases of method development, testing, and adoption. It also recognized the value of industrial support to enlarge the Association's financial base. A subcommittee on membership was formed by the Long Range Planning Committee, with industrial as well as official representation. Federal agencies supporting AOAC, and other segments of the membership, were asked to express their views on various new positions AOAC might take regarding industrial participation. These included enlarging the privileges of Associate Members and establishing an industry-sustaining member category for companies. The proposal for increased participation from industry was generally well received, and various suggestions for accomplishing it were proposed. In 1979 the Executive Committee, which had been following the efforts of the Long Range Planning Committee, requested the committee to develop a mechanism to permit industrial participation in the financial support of AOAC. At this time the coincidental appointment of a comptroller of AOAC provided for expert advice regarding the intricacies of collecting and handling the various types of funds, as well as for the revision of the Association's bookkeeping and accounting practices to be fully attuned to the rapid evolution of the Association.

As a result of Long Range Planning Committee recommendations and further deliberation by the Executive Committee, in 1980, a category of membership for Private Sustaining Members was added to that of Government Sustaining Members, which had been initiated as one of the responses to the Ritts Report. A Government Sustaining Member was defined as an agency of a local, state, provincial, or national government. Any other firm, business, or organization became eligible to be a Private Sustaining Member. The annual membership fee for the latter category was set at $500 and the enthusiastic response from industry was gratifying not only from a financial aspect but also because it indicated the esteem in which the regulated industries held AOAC activities. The Constitution was also changed at the same time to reflect the eligibility of Associate Members for official positions including committee members, General Referees, Associate Referees, and liaison representatives. In regard to the Committees on Official Methods, a restriction was included limiting the number of Associate Members on each committee to less than half, and specifying that the chairman must be a Member. Associate Members, since the Constitution change, have become welcome and valuable additions in those capacities and have added immeasurably to the successful pursuit of the AOAC mission. Also as a result of a Long Range Planning Committee recommendation, a major membership drive was launched beginning in 1979, using, among other things, an excellent printed brochure explaining AOAC purposes, aims, and functional operation. A new slide series with commentary depicting AOAC functions was also developed. Other actions advancing and solidifying the AOAC independent position at this time were the establishment of a committee to continue negotiations with FDA on cooperative agreements for the current and subsequent fiscal years, the establishment of a Ways and Means Committee and the appointment of the first full-time Assistant Executive Director, responsible for relations with Associate and General Referees and methods committee members. This new staff addition relieved the Executive Director of much routine work and greatly expedited the affairs of the AOAC office.

Regional Sections and State Participation

The formation of the first regional sections of AOAC in the early 1980s was a major accomplishment in the long campaign to reactivate and further stimulate the enthusiasm of experiment station, academic, and state regulatory chemists to participate more fully in the work and affairs of the Association and increase financial support from states and provinces.

In the earliest years of AOAC's existence, the major emphasis on fertilizer analysis, primarily a state responsibility, made the participation of state chemists essential, and they were the major force in establishing and sustaining the fledgling organization. Even though Wiley engineered federal support from almost the very beginning, the nonfederal members were the major participants in all phases of the Association's early activities. Several factors developed over the years to swing the balance toward a predominance of federally employed chemists.

Although the number of chemists employed by the states grew very rapidly after the passage of the Morrill Act in 1862 and the Hatch Act in 1887, and the subsequent establishment of agricultural experiment stations throughout the United States, the scope of responsibility of official chemists was limited by the regulations that evolved. These were, as previously mentioned, limited in most cases to fertilizer, and later to feeds and pesticides. In most instances, under a much simpler administrational structure than we have today, the officials charged with enforcing the regulatory laws were practicing analytical chemists who participated in method development and testing, as well as directly supervising other technical assistants. During this time the relatively small membership combined with the zeal of individual chemists to participate in the solution of their own problems acted to maintain an association where the contribution of the states was prominently evident.

The visibility of state participation was further enhanced by the formation in 1909 of the Association of American Feed Control Officials (AAFCO) which was initially organized to bring about uniformity in laws and regulations governing the distribution and sale of feeds in the various states. From its inception until the early 1960s, AAFCO held its meetings in connection with those of AOAC. There was a large overlap in membership and many state members would not have been able to attend both meetings if they were held separately. The organizations had much in common. The Collaborative Check Sample Program of AAFCO was initiated to monitor the efficiency and precison of feed control laboratories. Since AOAC collaborative studies were structured to test methods, the use of AOAC methods in the Collaborative Check Sample Program became a welcome corollary. References to selected feed analysis methods of AOAC were added to the AAFCO official publication in 1945. A cooperative study of feedstuff sampling was conducted by the two associations under the leadership of Dr. F. W. Quackenbush of Purdue and accepted as official in 1950. The interlocking membership enhanced the general cooperative effort. Many presidents of AOAC were also, at other times, president of AAFCO and other similar organizations with strong state representation.

The American Association of Fertilizer Control Officials was another state-oriented group which was organized in 1946. It provided a forum to discuss administrative control problems and announce the fertilizer control officials' objectives to the fertilizer industry and to American agriculture. As with the feed control officials, the fertilizer group, which changed its name to the Association of American Plant Food Officials in 1969, was interested in as much uniformity in the laws and regulations as practicable. The organizations had the whole-hearted support of industry toward this end. This Association also, from its very beginning, held its meetings in conjunction with the October annual convention of the AOAC, and many of its members attended the other meetings.

The above was also true of the American Association of Pest Control Officials, which began in 1947 and met during the week of the AOAC meetings at the same location as AOAC and the other control official associations. As each group came into existence, the schedule was modified to accommodate their sessions later in the week after a shortened AOAC meeting. Much valuable interaction was effected between the state officials and regulatory scientists and the industry representatives and scientists. The interaction among the associations was also very important. Many of the officials were chemists and had a strong interest in AOAC activities. The fertilizer and pesticide associations had also begun conducting check sample programs, and methodology was of prime importance to their programs.

The schedule of all four organizations meeting at the same hotel in Washington, DC, during the same week was maintained until 1961. The decision to separate was not a sudden or frivolous one. Agitation for such action was referred to as early as 1953 in Dr. Harry Fisher's presidential address. He praised the faithfulness of the control official associations to AOAC as the "mother organization" and their resistance to "occasional ill-advised efforts of a few of their members to have them go their separate ways." Limitations on the length of each meeting were becoming a serious problem, with some overlap and night sessions being necessary. An additional pressure was imposed on the control official associations by the regulated industries, especially feed manufacturers, for earlier announcement of official actions which might require label changes or other modifications to products before the annual January reregistration time. Industry maintained that under the existing time frame, necessary changes could not be made in time. Starting in 1961, the separation of the meetings of the control officials from that of the AOAC began. The advancement of feed and fertilizer control meetings to the week before the AOAC meeting and a concurrent increase in the total number of meeting days had the advantage of only one trip needed to attend all. The following year, the three official groups met in Cincinnati, Ohio, the week before AOAC, allowing for an extended trip which could still include all meetings.

However, at this time increased pressure from industry for earlier release of the *Feed Control Official Publication*, which detailed actions taken at the annual meeting affecting reregistration, became so strong that the control officials decided to move their meeting date to August. Since so many of the control officials held jurisdiction over more than one type of commodity, it would have been highly impractical to split the meetings of the three groups. Shifting the meeting time to August ended any possibility of coordination with the AOAC meeting and, hence, the necessity to meet in Washington.

The first August meeting was held in Salt Lake City, Utah, in 1963. It was decided that subsequent sessions would be held in various regions of the country, in hopes of getting better representation from the different regions. At this time, the separation resulting from such a shift in date and place for the control official meetings was more feasible than it would have been in earlier years because of changes in policies regarding regulatory enforcement and restructuring of regulatory agencies within many states. The regulatory functions of most agricultural colleges and experiment stations had been transferred to other state agencies, and the expansion of those functions had reached a point where many of the officials were no longer practicing analytical chemists. Consequently, the overlap in interest between the associations was not as great as it had been and a separation was less disruptive. Nevertheless, the shifting of the control officials associations' meetings did have a significant adverse affect on the balance of state participation in the affairs of AOAC compared to the federal activity, which had maintained a steady growth since Wiley began to increase the functions and staff of the USDA Bureau of Chemisty.

The passage of the original Food and Drug Act in 1906 had led to the rapid expansion in number of official analytical chemists in the federal government, as already mentioned. Subsequent federal laws, particularly the 1938 revision which became the Federal Food, Drug and Cosmetic Act, and a series of amendments, increased the number of government chemists and the scope of their interest enormously. Establishment of the Environmental Protection Agency, with its far-reaching analytical responsibilities, was another major factor in boosting the numbers of federally employed scientists with interest in the affairs of AOAC. The need for proven, legally acceptable methods to enforce federal laws and regulations mandated that close cooperation with AOAC be maintained. Support and participation by this sector of the profession became increasingly important and influential. Although the idea was suggested on several occasions, it was impractical to move the AOAC meeting to sites other than Washington in an effort to better interact with the control officials associations. It was felt that the loss of Washington area-based members would be too substantial.

Still, it was felt that lagging state interest and participation in AOAC studies was a serious problem, and in 1962, the Executive Committee authorized the president to establish a committee to assist in a study of federal, state, and local food and drug laws. The study was being conducted by the Public Administration Service (PAS) and the purpose of the AOAC committee was to urge PAS to emphasize the importance of laboratory analysis and methodology in their study of federal-state relations. The committee represented AOAC in the PAS Committee investigations. The PAS Committee report, released in 1965, pointed out the usefulness and value of AOAC methods and the Association's activities. The report also discussed some of the problems inherent in some state laboratories, which were attributed, in part, to narrowness of viewpoint and experience. These problems could be ameliorated by better communication and by attending meetings, conferences, and training sessions. Federal assistance, when needed, was also recommended. In response to the report, the Long Range Planning Committee recommended, in 1966, that area chapters should be established to secure more state participation in methodology studies. The committee also considered the idea of hiring a retired scientist knowledgeable in AOAC, to visit state agencies to promote more effort in methodology. Both of these turned out to be excellent suggestions when adopted at much later dates.

With the completion of the PAS Committee report, the Committee on Federal-States consultant group which had worked with the PAS Committee representing AOAC, was renamed, in 1967, the Committee on State Participation. The desirability of such a committee was supported by a Long Range Planning Committee report which showed that in 1967-68, 322 of the Associate Referees represented U.S. government agencies, 49 represented states, 107 represented industry, and nine represented the Canadian government. In its report in 1968, the Committee on State Participation presented a six-point program. This included compiling an inventory of states' needs and capabilities in areas served by the Association, the use of workshops in various states and regions to familiarize personnel with AOAC methods and method development activities, and establishing specific responsibilities regarding communication with state personnel.

The Committee on State Participation took the leadership in contacting prospective members. In 1972, it sent letters to each state official in charge of chemical or bacteriological laboratories in departments of agriculture, health departments or other pertinent jurisdictions, outlining reasons to show that state participation would be valuable to all concerned. Thirty-six states replied that they either were already participating or would participate in studies, when contacted by Referees or Associate Referees with specific problems. The committee followed up, in 1973, by contacting each state and territory laboratory with a request that they serve as collaborators. Again the response was good, with about 40 states indicating that they were participating in studies encompassing chemical and bacteriological methods. They also suggested that more could be done if the Referees approached them with specific assignments. By 1974, with the increasing need to expand the base of financial support for AOAC's independent status, the activities of the committee were broadened to help in developing contracts with state regulatory departments and Canadian provinces.

In 1974, with the help of the Executive Committee and Glenn Kilpatrick of FDA, the Committee on State Participation succeeded in having a resolution passed in support of AOAC at the annual convention of the National Association of State Departments of Agriculture (NASDA). The resolution encouraged state departments of agriculture to contribute financial support to AOAC in anticipation of the following increased services to state control agencies: local area meetings; special training; leadership in the development of methodology; and development of quality assurance and analyst proficiency programs. The following year, NASDA adopted a resolution approving a formula for funding AOAC by individual states, based on population and number of agencies involved. The committee continued its efforts to enlist additional states in AOAC support and to improve communications and cooperation. In 1977, the Committee suggested that alternate meetings be held at Washington, DC, and at other sites around the country. This proposal, which had been made several times previously by others, was still not acceptable because of the large member population in the Washington area. The subsequent initiation of spring workshops, in 1976, provided a partial solution.

At this time, the chairman of the Committee on State Participation, Eugene Holeman of Tennessee, began his assignment as states liaison representative to make personal contacts with state commissioners and laboratory directors on a part-time basis. Mr. Holeman was very active in this role and succeeded in securing substantial state funding for AOAC. After his subsequent retirement from the committee in 1978, Mr. Holeman continued his activity as AOAC liaison representative to the states.

Meanwhile, the committee continued its attempts to determine what problems existed in getting full and enthusiastic state support of AOAC through the use of surveys and special meetings with state officials at the annual convention. In 1980, the name of the committee was changed to the State and Provincial Participation Committee, recognizing the valuable part Canada had played in the Association, and the importance of maintaining and increasing its interest in AOAC. In its 1981 report, the committee endorsed the idea of regional groups to help satisfy the need felt by states and provinces for a system to bring their laboratories into closer contact with the Association.

In 1978, the Long Range Planning Committee had reactivated its 1966 recommendation, suggesting that the possibility of establishing local sections be considered in the future. The following year, it reported that several approaches for regional sections would be developed in 1980. Then, in 1980, the Membership Subcommittee of the Long Range Planning Committee drew up plans for the establishment of regional sections of Association members. Such sections were to meet periodically to take part in programs of interest to the involved membership in the given areas. Pilot studies in the Pacific Northwest United States and/or Washington, DC, were suggested. This proposal was adopted by the Board of Directors at the annual meeting. In 1981, at the request of the Board of Directors, the Long Range Planning Committee began to develop concepts for model bylaws for regional sections to be given to the Constitution Committee for specific drafting.

The Pacific Northwest Section became the first regional section, in 1981, when it met and attracted 85 attendees. The attendance at the second Pacific Northwest meeting increased to 120, supporting the optimistic view that regional sections were an idea whose time had come. The attendance comprised a cross section of persons concerned with commodity regulation and included state laboratory directors, federal personnel, section heads, laboratory managers, chemists, and technicians. These meetings afforded the first opportunity in many cases for the bench chemist and technician to attend such a gathering. Many of those who came were not familiar at all with AOAC or its functions. This regional section and the others which have newly organized have shown great promise as vehicles to extend the support of AOAC in the states, and solve the very serious problem existing in AOAC for some time--that of sufficiently increasing the number of collaboratively studied and adopted methods to satisfy the steadily increasing demand.

What's In A Name

A subject which continues to occupy the attention of AOAC is the name of the Association. As early as 1898, at the fifteenth annual convention, President A. L. Winton observed in his presidential address, "The name under which we are known gives little idea of our purpose and work." He explained that he felt the Association consisted of a group of agricultural analysts, and that perhaps the designation of agricultural chemists was too broad. He also felt that, "There is no immediate prospect that a further expansion of our work will be found advisable." Although the prophesy of non-expansion was to be proven wrong almost immediately, the concern over the name of the organization has been voiced by others over the years. However, the problem soon became one of the name failing to include a large sector of the membership, rather than being too broad. The expansion of AOAC into non-agricultural areas was recognized by former President C. A. Browne when he proposed, in 1927, that the name be changed to "Association of Official and Agricultural Chemists," which would retain the initials AOAC. There was some support for a name change at that time, but no action was taken.

In 1955, a proposal was made in the Executive Committee to change the name to "Association of Official Analytical Chemists," or "Association of Official and Analytical Chemists" to more accurately describe the membership at that time. A Committee on Change in Name of the Association was appointed with Secretary/Treasurer Emeritus Henry Lepper as chairman. In the first committee report, Lepper gave an excellent review of the historical significance of the name, relating the events and changes which had occurred to affect its pertinence. He explained that in the early days of AOAC, when agricultural chemistry was taught as an entity in many colleges, the agricultural chemist was a recognized specialist. Most of the founders and early members had been agricultural chemists who engaged in agricultural research as well as regulatory activities. As the scope of regulatory activites expanded beyond agricultural products, it was recognized that regulatory enforcement was not a true agricultural function. Much of that function was vested in newly established state regulatory agencies or departments of health rather than agricultural experiment stations or agriculture departments. This development, coupled with the broad increase in disciplines represented in the membership, gave rise to the question of the appropriateness of "Agricultural" in the name of the Association.

The Committee on Change in Name recognized that a name change would be in order, but pointed out that the initials AOAC should be retained. It did not propose a specific name, however, and cautioned that before any change in name was undertaken, the members should have an opportunity to consider it and offer suggestions. In response, the Executive Committee requested the Secretary to poll the active members of the Association to determine their sentiments regarding a name change, and to determine what difficulties, legal and other, might be involved in effecting a change. The poll showed an absence of a preponderance of sentiment for a change, and since the name change committee felt that they could not conceive of a truly appropriate name retaining "AOAC," they did not recommend a change. They felt that the name had "the weight of heritage and the work of sentiment and prestige to commend it" and recommended the retention of "Association of Official Agricultural Chemists." The Executive Committee approved this second and final report of the committee. No further action was taken until 1962, when the Executive Committee again authorized the president to appoint a committee to consider a change in the name of the Association, still retaining the AOAC initials because of their legal significance. Since many laws and the uniform bills referred specifically to methods of the "Association of Official Agricultural Chemists," they would have to be amended to include the new name. Some referred only to AOAC and would require no action in the event of a change retaining those initials.

The subject had been resurrected and discussed by the Committee on Improvement. They urged the Executive Committee to again investigate the possibility of finding a more descriptive substitute for the outmoded name. In 1965, the Committee on Change in Name of AOAC, chaired by Stacy B. Randle, unanimously recommended to the Executive Committee that the designation AOAC be retained, but the name of the organization be changed to Association of Official Analytical Chemists, citing the reasons already discussed. The Executive Committee adopted the recommendation, and the appropriate Constitutional change was made. Although this simple change was quite acceptable and eliminated the outmoded restriction of "agricultural," it did not recognize in the name of the Association the large and important contingent of members who were not analytical chemists.

In his presidential address in 1970, Dr. Banes proposed that, in order to include all the disciplines and geographical areas in the Association designation, the name be changed to the International Association of Official Analytical Chemists and Collaborating Scientists, retaining the abbreviated letter designation of AOAC. The suggestion was apparently not pursued, but the issue of the name was not yet settled. The problems of survival of the AOAC posed by the Ritts Committee report were more important than a name change during the next decade, but as the centennial meeting of AOAC approached, attention was again focused in that direction. In 1981, the Board of Directors requested the president to announce a contest to revise the name of the Association to incorporate all scientists and still maintain the AOAC acronym. The judges of the contest were to be the members of the AOAC staff, and the prize was an all-expense-paid trip to the 1984 Spring Training Workshop in Philadelphia. At the October 1983 annual meeting, the winning entry, Association of Official Analytical Communities, was announced, but no official action was taken.

As the New Century Begins

Revolutionary developments have occurred in the past century in the areas of analytical chemistry, consumer product regulation, environmental protection, and consumer protection legislation, and in AOAC itself. Despite these, some things have not changed. The Association has not wavered from its historical position that an analytical method is not acceptable as "official" until it has passed the test of collaborative study by a group of reliable analysts in individual laboratories. Participating collaborators, Associate Referees, Referees, and committee members still contribute their time and effort on a voluntary basis, with the blessings of their employers and supervisors. AOAC methods are still respected as definitive when data obtained by using such methods are presented as testimony in litigation. Some of the earliest problems are also present. For example, Harvey Wiley would be chagrined, if not surprised, to learn that the Food and Drug Administration was directed by Act of Congress in April 1983 to desist from banning the use of saccharin as an artificial sweetener for at least two more years. Wiley's battle against saccharin began in the very early 1900s; despite modern scientific evidence that it can cause cancer in laboratory animals, his victory has not yet been totally achieved.

Though the basic goals and objectives remained strong all through the first 100 years, they were, as we have seen, broadened beyond the most ambitious aspirations of the founders. Major challenges to analytical methodology accompanied each new consumer protection law or revision. One such instance was the increased need for research and adoption of methods for the detection of filth, in the early 1940s, in response to the need to enforce the revised Food, Drug and Cosmetic Act. A section on detection of extraneous matter added to *Official Methods of Analysis* at that time relied heavily on the work of such AOAC members as B.J. Howard, who devised the Howard mold count procedure, and J.D. Wildman, who developed simple methods of estimating the amount of mold mycelium in cream. His device, the Wildman trap flask, is still standard equipment for isolation of many extraneous materials. We have already mentioned how the legislation regulating pesticide residues, environmental pollutants, and similar contaminants helped trigger the demand for methods sensitive in the trace residue region; such methods naturally required more sophisticated instrumentation. Innovative instrumentation in which computers are used in an increasing number of ways will certainly be an important component of AOAC's second century of official methods.

Liaison with other analytical organizations both in North America and elsewhere continues to be of vital importance to the success of AOAC. The March 1983 issue of the AOAC Journal listed liaison representatives to more than 60 associations, agencies, committees, and subcommittees which share common interests with AOAC. They function in the United States, Canada, and many other countries. This ongoing cooperation for the development and exchange of methodology and information has proved invaluable in preventing duplication of effort and proliferation of methodology, and in encouraging harmonization of studies. The importance placed on the international meeting for harmonization of collaborative studies held in conjunction with the AOAC centennial meeting illustrates the strong desire for continued cooperation.

The relatively new independence of the Association has been a successful undertaking, thus far. AOAC will continue to maintain its traditional strong bonds to federal, state, and provincial regulatory agencies. They are still prime users and prime suppliers of the methods of interest to AOAC, and they supply much volunteer assistance for collaborator and referee assignments. Also, the monetary support, primarily in the form of contracts, still provides a substantial and ongoing portion of the budget. At the same time, AOAC has been able to appreciably broaden its base of support by increasing the participation of industry representatives in almost all spheres of activity, including financial sustenance.

Financial problems still exist, perhaps more pressing than ever. AOAC's scope of activities and consequent needs have escalated with its growth and recent independent status. While the Journal, *Official Methods of Analysis*, publishing services, and memberships provide much monetary support, agency contracts are still a mainstay. Since these are subject to the exigencies of public budgets and the fluctuations in emphasis on the varying regulatory aspects of any particular agency at any time, a Ways and Means Committee was designated in 1982 to study and recommend possible solutions to special fiscal problems as well as ways to establish a more permanent financial base for some of AOAC's activities.

Major challenges still exist also in the area of official methods adoptions, AOAC's raison d'etre. The rate of scientific and technological advancement has surpassed the speed at which methods can be developed, much less collaboratively studied, with the resources generally available. Budget constraints in all branches of government, as well as industry, have led to severe limitations in the time allotted for participation in methods development and collaborative studies, unless the methods are of immediate interest to the proposed sponsor. This becomes a particular problem in some cases, since there has been a tendency of some agencies, in the face of limited resources, to adopt a policy of downgrading the economic fraud regulatory function in favor of hazard regulatory functions focused on health risks. As a consequence of the unavoidable delay in adopting official methods for the very large number of new chemicals of all kinds for which tests are needed, AOAC has been under much pressure to consider making available various stop-gap procedures to supplement fully collaborated official methods of analysis. Some methods of speeding up availability of analytical procedures without sacrificing the integrity of AOAC official methods must be devised. This is certainly one of the most critical problems for the new century, and the answer may be a most important factor in determining the extent of AOAC's continuing influence in the analytical methods community.

As the Association of Official Analytical Chemists inaugurates its second 100 years, it looks back at a proud century of growth, service, and accomplishment in supplying the tools to protect our food, our health, and our environment: "A century of analytical excellence." AOAC looks forward to the next 100 years of using new, undreamed-of technology to continue to help solve the age-old problem of consumer protection.

Bibliography

(1) Anderson, O.E., Jr (1958) *The Health of a Nation*, University of Chicago Press, Chicago, IL

(2) Ambruster, H.W. (1935) *Why Not Enforce the Laws We Have?* Private Printing

(3) Davis, J.S. (1949) *Carl Alsberg--Scientist at Large*, Stanford University Press, Palo Alto, CA

(4) Lamb, R. de F. (1936) *American Chamber of Horrors*, Grosset & Dunlap, New York, NY

(5) Filby, F.A. (1934) *A History of Food Adulteration & Analysis*, G. Allen & Unwin Ltd, London, UK

(6) Fuller, J.G. (1972) *200,000,000 Guinea Pigs*, G.P. Putnam & Sons, New York, NY

(7) Hemphill, J. (1962) *Fruitcake & Arsenic*, Little, Brown & Company, Boston, MA, & Toronto, Canada

(8) Kallet, A., & Schlink, F.J. (1933) *100,000,000 Guinea Pigs*, Grosset & Dunlap, New York, NY

(9) Lucas, S. (1978) *The FDA*, Celestial Arts, Milbrae, CA

(10) MacLeod, R., & Collins, P. (1981) *The Parliament of Science*, Science Reviews, London, UK

(11) Morrell, J., & Thackery, A. (1981) *Gentlemen of Science: Early Years of the British Association for the Advancement of Science*, Oxford University Press, Oxford, UK

(12) Turner, J.S. (1970) *The Chemical Feast*, Grossman Publishers, New York, NY

(13) Wiley, H.W. (1930) *Harvey W. Wiley, An Autobiography*, The Bobbs Merrill Co., Indianapolis, IN

(14) Wiley, H.W. (1930; reprinted 1976) *History of a Crime Against the Food Law*, Arno Press, New York, NY

C.W. Dabney, Jr, Secretary 1885
State Chemist of North Carolina and
Assistant Secretary, U.S. Dept of
Agriculture

C. Richardson, Secretary 1886–1889
Assistant Chief, Chemistry Division,
U.S. Dept of Agriculture

H.W. Wiley, Secretary 1890–1912
Chief, U.S. Bureau of Chemistry

W.D. Bigelow, Secretary/Treasurer
1912–1913
Assistant Chief, U.S. Bureau of
Chemistry

C.L. Alsberg, Secretary/Treasurer
1914–1920
Chief, U.S. Bureau of Chemistry

R.W. Balcom, Secretary/Treasurer
1921
U.S. Food, Drug and Insecticide
Administration

W.W. Skinner, Secretary/Treasurer
1922–1939, 1941–1944
Assistant Chief, U.S. Bureau of
Chemistry

H.A. Lepper, Secretary/Treasurer 1940,
1945–1952
U.S. Food and Drug Administration

William Horwitz, Executive Director
1953–1979
U.S. Food and Drug Administration

D.B. MacLean, Executive Director
1980–
Association of Official Analytical
Chemists

Winners of the Harvey W. Wiley Award

1957   Lloyd C. Mitchell, Food and Drug Administration
1958   Kenneth D. Jacob, U.S. Department of Agriculture
1959   Francis A. Gunther, University of California
1960   Jonas Carol, Food and Drug Administration
1961   Paul A. Clifford, Food and Drug Administration
1962   Milton S. Schechter, U.S. Department of Agriculture
1963   O'Dean L. Kurtz, Lauhoff Grain Company, and Kenton L. Harris,
         Food and Drug Administration (joint award)
1964   John B. Smith, University of Rhode Island
1965   Forrest W. Quackenbush, Purdue University
1966   J. Alexander Campbell, Canada Food and Drug Directorate
1967   Robert T. O'Connor, U.S. Department of Agriculture
1968   Daniel Banes, Food and Drug Administration
1969   C.O. Willits, U.S. Department of Agriculture
1970   Morton Beroza, U.S. Department of Agriculture
1971   Charles W. Gehrke, University of Missouri
1972   Clyde L. Ogg, U.S. Department of Agriculture
1973   Joseph Levine, Food and Drug Administration
1974   Dale M. Coulson, Stanford Research Institute
1975   William Horwitz, Food and Drug Administration
1976   Walter A. Pons, Jr, U.S. Department of Agriculture
1977   Gunter Zweig, Environmental Protection Agency
1978   Bernard E. Saltzman, University of Cincinnati
1979   W. Perce McKinley, Health and Welfare Canada
1980   Yeshajahu Pomeranz, U.S. Department of Agriculture
1981   Leonard Stoloff, Food and Drug Administration
1982   Odette L. Shotwell, U.S. Department of Agriculture
1983   Velmer A. Fassel, Ames Laboratory

Honorary Members

1912   Harvey W. Wiley, Honorary President
1921   E.F. Ladd
1956   H.A. Huston
1957   Henry A. Lepper
1961   Paul B. Dunbar
1981   William Horwitz

Past Presidents of AOAC

1885	S.W. Johnson, Connecticut Experiment Station, New Haven, CT
1886	H.W. Wiley, U.S. Department of Agriculture, Washington, DC
1887	E.H. Jenkins, Connecticut Agriculture Experiment Station, New Haven, CT
1888	P.E. Chazal, State Chemist of South Carolina, Columbia, SC
1889	J.A. Myers, West Virginia Agricultural Experiment Station, Morgantown, WV
1890	M.A. Scovell, Kentucky Agricultural Experiment Station, Lexington, KY
1891	G.C. Caldwell, New York Agricultural Experiment Station, Ithaca, NY
1892	N.T. Lupton, Alabama Agricultural Experiment Station, AL
1893	S.M. Babcock, University of Wisconsin, Madison, WI
1894	E.B. Voorhees, New Jersey Agricultural Experiment Station, New Brunswick, NJ
1895	H.A. Huston, State Chemist of Indiana, Lafayette, IN
1896	B.B. Ross, State Chemist of Alabama, Auburn, AL
1897	W. Frear, Agricultural Experiment Station, State College, PA
1898	A.L. Winton, Agricultural Experiment Station, New Haven, CT
1899	R.C. Kedzie, Agricultural Experiment Station, Agricultural College, MI
1900	B.W. Kilgore, State Chemist, Raleigh, NC
1901	L.L. Van Slyke, Agricultural Experiment Station, Geneva, NY
1902	H.J. Wheeler, Agricultural Experiment Station, Kingston, RI
1903	R.J. Davidson, Agricultural Experiment Station, Blacksburg, VA
1904	M.E. Jaffa, Agricultural Experiment Station, Berkeley, CA
1905	C.L. Penny, Agricultural Experiment Station, Newark, DE
1906	C.G. Hopkins, Agricultural Experiment Station, Urbana, IL
1907	J.P. Street, Agricultural Experiment Station, New Haven, CT
1908	H. Snyder, Agricultural Experiment Station, St. Anthony Park, MN
1909	W.D. Bigelow, U.S. Department of Agriculture, Washington, DC
1910	W.A. Withers, Agricultural Experiment Station, Raleigh, NC
1911	F.W. Woll, Agricultural Experiment Station, Madison, WI
1912	H.J. Patterson, Maryland Agricultural College, College Park, MD

1913   G.S. Fraps, Agricultural Experiment Station, College Station,
         TX
1914   E.F. Ladd, Agricultural Experiment Station, Agricultural
         College, ND
1915   C.H. Jones, Agricultural Experiment Station, Burlington, VT
1916   R.N. Brackett, Clemson College, Clemson, SC
1917-8   J.K. Haywood, U.S. Department of Agriculture, Washington,
         DC
1919   P.F. Trowbridge, Agricultural Experiment Station, Agricultural
         College, ND
1920   H.C. Lythgoe, State Department of Health, Boston, MA
1921   W.F. Hand, Mississippi Agricultural and Mechanical College,
         MS
1922   F.P. Veitch, U.S. Department of Agriculture, Washington, DC
1923   A.J. Patten, Agricultural Experiment Station, East Lansing, MI
1924   R.E. Doolittle, Food and Drug Inspection Station, Chicago, IL
1925   C.A. Browne, U.S. Department of Agriculture, Washington,
         DC
1926   W.W. Randall, State of Maryland Department of Health,
         Baltimore, MD
1927   W.H. MacIntire, University of Tennessee, Knoxville, TN
1928   O. Schreiner, U.S. Department of Agriculture, Washington,
         DC
1929   H.B. McDonnell, Agricultural Experiment Station, College
         Park, MD
1930   E.M. Bailey, Agricultural Experiment Station, New Haven, CT
1931   H.D. Haskins, Agricultural Experiment Station, Amherst, MA
1932   A.E. Paul, Food and Drug Administration, Chicago, IL
1933   J.W. Kellogg, Department of Agriculture, Harrisburg, PA
1934   R. Harcourt, Ontario Agricultural College, Guelph, Ontario,
         Canada
1935   F.C. Blanck, U.S. Department of Agriculture, Washington, DC
1936   H.H. Hanson, State Board of Agriculture, Dover, DE
1937   C.C McDonnell, Food and Drug Administration, Washington,
         DC
1938   H.R. Kraybill, Purdue University, Lafayette, IN
1939   W.S. Frisbie, Food and Drug Administration, Washington, DC
1940   W.W. Skinner, U.S. Department of Agriculture, Washington,
         DC
1941   L.B. Broughton, University of Maryland, College Park, MD
1942-3   J.W. Sale, Food and Drug Administration, Washington, DC
1944   G.G. Frary, State Chemical Laboratory, Vermillion, SD
1945-6   W.H. Ross, U.S. Department of Agriculture, Beltsville, MD

1947	J.O. Clarke, Food and Drug Administration, Chicago, IL
1948	G.H. Marsh, Alabama Department of Agriculture and Industries, Montgomery, AL
1949	L.S. Walker, Agricultural Experiment Station, Burlington, VT
1950	W.A. Queen, Food and Drug Administration, Chicago, IL
1951	H.A. Halvorson, Department of Agriculture, Dairy, and Food, St. Paul, MN
1952	H.A. Lepper, Food and Drug Administration, Washington, DC
1953	H.J. Fisher, Connecticut Agricultural Experiment Station, New Haven, CT
1954	E.L. Griffin, U.S. Department of Agriculture, Washington, DC
1955	W.F. Reindollar, State Department of Health, Baltimore, MD
1956	K.D. Jacob, U.S. Department of Agriculture, Beltsville, MD
1957	M.P. Etheredge, Mississippi State College, State College, MS
1958	F.A. Vorhes, Food and Drug Administration, Washington, DC
1959	A.H. Robertson, State Food Laboratory, Albany, NY
1960	J. B. Smith, University of Rhode Island, Kingston, RI
1961	C.O. Willits, U.S. Department of Agriculture, Philadelphia, PA
1962	K.L. Milstead, Food and Drug Administration, Washington, DC
1963	F.W. Quackenbush, Purdue University, Lafayette, IN
1964	C.V. Marshall, Canada Department of Agriculture, Ottawa, Ontario, Canada
1965	M.S. Oakley, State Department of Health, Baltimore, MD
1966	S.B. Randle, New Jersey Agricultural Experiment Station, New Brunswick, NJ
1967	A.P. Mathers, Internal Revenue Service, Washington, DC
1968	B. Poundstone, Kentucky Agricultural Experiment Station, Lexington, KY
1969	D. Banes, Food and Drug Administration, Washington, DC
1970	L.S. Stuart, U.S. Department of Agriculture, Washington, DC
1971	H.A. Davis, University of New Hampshire, Durham, NH
1972	L.L. Ramsey, Food and Drug Administration, Washington, DC
1973	D.J. Mitchell, State Chemical Laboratory, Vermillion, SD
1974	F.M. Garfield, Drug Enforcement Administration, Washington, DC
1975	I. Hoffman, National Research Council of Canada, Ottawa, Ontario, Canada
1976	E.A. Epps, Jr, Louisiana State University, Baton Rouge, LA
1977	W.W. Wright, Food and Drug Administration, Washington, DC

1978	A.J. Malanoski, U.S. Department of Agriculture, Washington, DC
1979	E.D. Schall, Purdue University, West Lafayette, IN
1980	W.P. McKinley, Health and Welfare Canada, Ottawa, Ontario, Canada
1981	H.L. Reynolds, Food and Drug Administration, Washington, DC
1982	J.P. Minyard, Jr, State Chemical Laboratory, Mississippi State, MS
1983	W.R. Bontoyan, Environmental Protection Agency, Beltsville, MD
1984	C.W. Gehrke, University of Missouri, Columbia, MO

INDEX